"*Guerrilla Marketing for Coaches* shakes the traditional foundation that coaches have built their practice on. Jay Conrad Levinson and Andrew Neitlich bring to the professional industry creative, powerful, and brilliant insights that, if followed, will result in a million-dollar practice."

—**Jim Reilly**, Keys to the Business

"Andrew delivers, yet again, with what could literally become the coaching book of the century; so if you absolutely, positively want to succeed in coaching, then buy this book!"

—**Wayne Morris**, Eventus Coaching

"Andrew has given me the information that I desperately needed to clear out the clutter and replace them with strategies to move my business in the right direction and with the right mind frame in place to execute my new strategies. As a solopreneur, my biggest obstacle is not having a giant marketing department behind me, dedicated to selling my business or me. This is where Andrew came in, and here I am working towards mastering these strategies."

—**Sean**, Owner, SPT

"Jay Conrad Levinson and Andrew Neitlich take you on a journey that not only helps you to understand how to create a coaching practice, but also develops your thinking as a business owner. The title of their introduction tells you something about their thinking in this book, 'If coaching is booming, then why are so many coaches struggling to get by?' In other words, they are not afraid to ask the tough questions, as well as offer their insights as to possible answers. The book is filled with practical suggestions as well as keen insights on how to build, work, and sustain a coaching practice. Many business books offer ideas about how to build a business. This Guerrilla approach helps to get beneath those ideas and figure out how to make it really work. Definitely worth your time to study."

—**Robert Hockin**, Ph.D.

"*Guerrilla Marketing for Coaches* is more than a marketing blueprint—it's a six-step Business Building Bible for Coaches. Buy it, read it, do it and you will maximize results for your clients, colleagues and your career!"

—**Bill Lang**, Creator of the "Scores on the Board – Skill Building System" and Principal, The Human Performance Company

"Whether you're an experienced coach or one just starting out, Andrew Neitlich and Jay Conrad Levinson's *Guerrilla Marketing for Coaches* is a must-read. The book is a step-by-step guide for coaches who are serious about success. As a member of Andrew's Center for Executive Coaching, I have used the principles they teach in *Guerrilla Marketing for Coaches* to accelerate my own success as well as the success of the clients I coach. If you've been looking for something to help your coaching career take off, this is it. I only wish I had this information ten years ago!"

—**Joanie Natalizio**, Defero Business Coaching, LLC

"The writing and central focus of Andrew's work compels us all to take an introspective journey of self-discovery. This book helps you overcome the inherent fear of such a choice to pursue your own dreams with a proven model for success. If you learn from what Andrew is teaching and apply it diligently and passionately in your own life and professional practice, you cannot fail to achieve the goals and objectives you set for yourself. The simple power of his proven methods will fuel your passion, expand your vision, and drive your willingness to take the necessary risks in your own pursuit of performance excellence."

—**Michael E. Frisina**, Ph.D., Principal, The Frisina Group

"This book is the toolkit and roadmap to a seven-figure income! The wealth of information—including step-by-step processes—is coming from somebody who has been there and done it all. The most experienced coach will harvest many valuable tips, and the upcoming coach won't be able to put it down. Earmark it, highlight it, and take action!"

—**Helena Nyman**, President Executive Center of Excellence, www.ExecutiveCenterofExcellence.com

"This book has a wealth of information for someone who wants to take the next step with their coaching or consulting business. You provide a comprehensive view of what it takes to make it in this industry. Great book!"

—**Deborah Burgesser,** Principal Business Consultant, Executive Steps LLC, www.ExecutiveSteps.com

"Andrew Neitlich shows you how to clearly and proudly market yourself after identifying *your* unique qualities. Clarifying your marketing message and learning how to position yourself for success is extremely exciting, and the reward is great. With renewed confidence I'm taking the next step, resisting the urge to be all things to all people, and taking my business toward the next step of being prosperous for the long term."

—**Katie Miller**, Business Coach and also the founder of Katie's Cookies

"*Guerrilla Marketing for Coaches* is for real. While there are books about how to be a coach, there are very few that clearly depict how to create a real coaching business. Jay and Andrew excel at distilling the important information on creating a coaching business into a concrete set of actions to achieve success. If you are ready to create a sustaining and highly profitable coaching business, this is the guidebook."

—**Michael Wm. Dann**, CFP, Business and Leadership Coach, Bold In Life, LLC

"Andrew Neitlich is not only a coach's coach, but an individual who truly inspires his clients. He lives, breathes and completely understands the steps necessary to be a professional business coach. *Guerrilla Marketing for Coaches* is designed to help you differentiate yourself from the multitudes. Coaching is a highly personal and individual choice; by helping coaches understand what makes them unique, they can then become more of an effective resource for their clients. If you are ready to have the practice you thought of when you started, then read *Guerrilla Marketing for Coaches* now; then get ready to be inspired by one of the best."

—**Thom Torode**, MBA, CBC, President, Action Business Coaching & Development, Inc., Managing Director, Sunrise Capital Group, LLC, www.Coachthom.biz

"Well done! Purely a masterpiece; Andrew and Jay you have done it again. *Guerrilla Marketing for Coaches* is a must-read for anyone trying to take their coaching practice to the next level. Andrew and Jay spell it out for you step by step—with a no-nonsense approach and a straight path to success. Andrew: I continue to build my practice on everything you have taught me through your words and coaching. Your approach is direct, one that I think every coach can appreciate. Thank you for continuing to put out educational materials that give coaches a formula for success. This book will definitely be one that I keep near and dear to me."

—**Jason Baer**, Executive, Sales and Business Coaching,
Precision Winning, www.precisionwinning.com

"Andrew Neitlich and Jay Conrad Levinson's new book *Guerrilla Marketing for Coaches* is a much-needed, directional breath of fresh air. As an Executive Wellness Coach, I often tell my clients how important it is to stay motivated and focused on specific goals for success and results. This book cleverly does this for coaches in a concise and brilliant way. With a laser focus and inspiration, it serves as a success compass for coaches of all denominations. The authors leave no stone unturned when it comes to marketing and achieving a 'million dollar' coaching practice. I'm already integrating these tactics into my own business and helping other coaches find answers by sharing Neitlich and Levinson's proven strategies. I highly recommend that all coaches treat themselves and their coaching practice to this amazing book!"

—**Rick Osborn**, Executive Wellness Coach, RickOsborn.com

"Highly recommended! A MUST-read for all coaches looking to shift their business into high gear. This book is a blueprint for long-term success."

—**Richard Pierce**, six-time business owner and
Principal @ BusinessCoachLLC.com

"I loved this book! I've read many marketing books for coaches over the years, and Andrew Neitlich's *Guerrilla Marketing for Coaches* is by far the best. It's the one I'll be recommending to colleagues."

—**Barbra Sundquist**, www.WriteABio.com

"*Guerrilla Marketing for Coaches* is a must-have for people who want to be 'rock star' coaches. This book demystifies the path to prosperity, providing a powerful blueprint for a more rewarding experience as a coach. This book is powerful, accessible and, most importantly, empowers the reader to take action.

Thank you to Andrew and Jay Conrad for so generously sharing proven strategies and tactics to raise the bar on being a successful coach."

—**Kelley Black**, Founder & Managing Director, Balancing the Executive Life

"Andrew is refreshing in his ability to present the facts while keeping the reader captivated, on the edge of my seat for the next tool that will catapult my business growth into an entirely new realm, all the while unveiling my unique style. He maps vision into actionable steps that anyone might follow to success. Reading *Guerrilla Marketing for Coaches* is like watching your favorite game show and winning."

—**Ginger Reid**; Principal, EnterUp, LLC, www.enter-up.com

"*Guerrilla Marketing for Coaches* provides a pragmatic path that clearly establishes both the 'what' and the 'how' of creating, maintaining and exiting a successful coaching practice. While there are certainly numerous gems to be mined from this book, the most powerful may be the page dedicated to claiming your power as a coach. Read it first, read it often and then follow the road map Andrew provides in this book and you will claim both your power and the rewards associated with being a highly successful coach."

—**Jeffrey G. Soper**, Ph.D., Partner, LIPPartners and Author of *Making HR CLICK: Critical Skills for the New Talent Practice*

"Refreshingly crisp, genuine, and useful, Andrew Neitlich's new book *Guerrilla Marketing for Coaches* sets the standard for everyone else. While other books offer theories and general ideas, Neitlich's tour de force actually shows you how to set up a sustainable and lucrative living as a coach. Chapter 6's directive on developing a compelling marketing message is alone worth the price of the book. I'm living proof. This book's bountiful resources and step-by-step marketing process propelled me from start-up to six figures in less than 14 months. Keep it handy. You will reach for this book over and over again as you build and solidify your coaching practice."

—**Lorinda Clausen**, Founder and President, People Strategy Advisors

"Masterfully done! This book is an absolutely brilliant work, providing step-by-step, no-nonsense, insightful and intuitive information. *Guerrilla Marketing for Coaches* provides you with all the tools, tips, and techniques necessary to engage immediately and stops short of actually doing the work for you."

—**T.M. Dickens**, President, CEO, DICKENS Consulting Group LLC

"Every coach or consultant, for that matter, can benefit greatly from the ideas shared in this book. I've used quite a few with fantastic results so far, and the momentum will only continue to grow. If you're serious about building a successful and financially lucrative practice—a practice that can be worth 7 or 8 figures—then this book is a must-read."

—**Justin Cauley**, Business Enhancement & Value Maximization Expert, www.profitmaxsolutions.com

"This is a must-read for anyone looking to build a strong practice, from foundation to leverage and beyond! This book provides a six-step blueprint to develop a solid marketing program that will ensure that you will never miss an ideal opportunity for growth. *Guerrilla Marketing for Coaches* delivers all of the strategies to help any coach establish the practice of his/her dreams!"

—**Angela L. Edwards**, President & CEO, Castle Thunder Technologies, www.castlethunder.com

"Wow—magnificent insights! *Guerrilla Marketing for Coaches* is a great resource for all coaches at any level in their career to guide you in creating an innovative boost to new and current programs you offer as a coach. The real-life case studies and examples show you what works and what does not work. Jay Levinson and Andrew Neitlich have created another masterpiece!"

—**Charlene Mallay**, Principal/Founder, Executive Edgeworks, www.execedgeworks.com

"The content is as amazing, practical and profitable as the coaching services that Andrew provides. By applying only a few of them, I was able to increase my revenues by almost 150% and learn how to focus my services to help my customers to increase their quality of life, competitiveness and, what is the ultimate benefit for them, their profitability."

—**Marco A. Nájera Sixto**; Strategist, Coach and Consultant at Grupo LORMAR

GUERRILLA MARKETING FOR COACHES

Six Steps to Building Your
MILLION-DOLLAR COACHING PRACTICE

JAY CONRAD LEVINSON
& ANDREW NEITLICH

Guerrilla Marketing Press
an imprint of Morgan James Publishing
New York

GUERRILLA MARKETING
FOR COACHES
Six Steps to Building Your
MILLION-DOLLAR COACHING PRACTICE

Jay Conrad Levinson & Andrew Neitlich

ISBN 978-1-61448-156-0 Paperback
ISBN 978-1-61448-157-7 eBook
Library of Congress Control Number: 2011939905

Published by:

Guerrilla Marketing Press
an imprint of Morgan James Publishing
The Entrepreneurial Publisher
5 Penn Plaza, 23rd Floor
New York City, New York 10001
(212) 655-5470 Office
(516) 908-4496 Fax
www.MorganJamesPublishing.com

Interior Design by:
Bonnie Bushman
bbushman@bresnan.net

In an effort to support local communities and raise awareness and funds, Morgan James Publishing donates one percent of all book sales for the life of each book to Habitat for Humanity.
To get involved today, visit
www.HelpHabitatForHumanity.org

ALSO BY
JAY CONRAD LEVINSON
AND ANDREW NEITLICH

Guerrilla Marketing for a Bulletproof Career: How to Attract Ongoing Opportunities in Perpetually Gut-Wrenching Times, for Entrepreneurs, Employees, and Everyone in Between

Guerrilla Marketing Job Escape Plan: The Ten Battles You Must Fight to Start Your Own Business, and How to Win Them Decisively

*For coaches who are serious
about building a successful practice*

ACKNOWLEDGMENTS

FROM JAY CONRAD LEVINSON

I owe heartfelt acknowledgment to Andrew Neitlich, who did all the heavy lifting and supplied the brilliance with which this book has been written. If you benefit from his insight, give all the credit to him, for I was merely along for the ride. My main contribution has been to provide the guerrilla spirit that has infused him. He has done a wonderful job absorbing it and spreading it to everyone who reads the words he has written.

FROM ANDREW NEITLICH

I remain forever grateful to Jim Reilly, who was generous enough to introduce me to Jay Conrad Levinson. Jay has been a hero of mine for decades, and it continues to be an honor and a highlight of my career to have this opportunity to work with him on a third book.

I am also extremely grateful to the members of The Center for Executive Coaching, Institute for Business Growth, and The Center for Career Coaching. I appreciate your generosity in sharing your stories about building your coaching firms. I am also awed by your persistence and commitment when it comes to building your coaching practices. You continue to raise the bar for the coaching profession, and it is a privilege to get to be able to work with you.

Special thanks to social media expert Crystal McCann of BambuSky for her guidance with the section about Internet marketing and social media. She has helped my wife and me with the social media efforts for our respective businesses, and I am grateful for her knowledge.

Of course, thanks always go to my wife, Elena. She is writing yet another book while I finish this one—except that she also manages to do the lion's share of work when it comes to getting the kids ready for school and extracurricular activities, keeping the house running smoothly, cooking gourmet meals, and running her own successful business. No married entrepreneur can succeed in business without a supportive spouse, and I am blessed that I am married to Elena. Finally, I want to acknowledge my children, Noah, Seth, and Willow, and wish them satisfaction, joy, peace, and success.

TABLE OF CONTENTS

Step I

LAY A SOLID STRATEGIC FOUNDATION

Step II

USE LOW-COST, HIGH-IMPACT TACTICS TO GET CLIENTS

Step III

CLOSE ENGAGEMENTS

Step IV

KEEP CLIENTS FOR LIFE, OR AT LEAST FOR A LONG TIME

Step V

BUILD A FIRM TO ENJOY LASTING WEALTH

Step VI

CREATE YOUR MILLION-DOLLAR BUSINESS PLAN

PREFACE
by Jay Conrad Levinson

Early pioneers blazed trails across our country, opening the American West and changing the personality of our nation permanently. Almost every day meant new passageways, rivers, valleys, waterfalls and mountain ranges. It sounds like a glorious experience discovering them. And it was.

But 10% of the pioneers died while making the journey. It wasn't as simple as it sounded and there were many pitfalls on the trails.

So it is with coaching. Coaching roared into existence in the middle of the last century and helped many people for many years. At the same time, it attracted people who were remarkably talented coaches. But as the industry has grown, so have the number of competitors. The level of complexity has risen noticeably. It's tougher now to earn a comfortable living through coaching than it has been in a long, long time. Want more bad news? It's only going to get tougher.

Want a generous supply of good news? The opportunities for coaching are more abundant than ever and the chances for financial superstardom have multiplied. Technology and psychology have combined to create methods and techniques for coaches to finally get what they've been dreaming about.

Andrew Neitlich put together this treasury of wisdom for coaches, along with methods of experiencing the superstardom I just mentioned.

This astonishing book lays it all out for you, clearly and uncomplicated, enticing and possible. It describes the potential journey from where you are today as a coach to where you could be if you knew all the inside tactics and strategies for prosperity. Those tactics and strategies await you in the upcoming pages.

With this book comes the new age of enlightenment for guerrillas. The earliest coaches, the pioneers in the field, did the best they could with the resources and knowledge at hand.

But those were the old days. Coaching was maturing and becoming more recognized, profound and available. That's why these new days require that coaches become aware of the new realities in coaching. They're all right here in this book.

Andrew takes you far beyond the realm of coaching. It has long been recognized that it's easier to deal with failure than with success. We're assuming you'll leave failure in the dust and begin to live a fulfilling life as a coach. Achieving the success this book can generate for you, what comes next for you?

There are lots to choose from. It will all be within your reach. Reading this book and doing what it suggests will separate the guerrilla readers from the ordinary readers. Anybody can read. Guerrillas excel at doing.

Just by owning this book and reading the preface proves that you're a doer. I'm betting on you.

Jay Conrad Levinson

DeBary, Florida

INTRODUCTION

IF COACHING IS BOOMING, WHY ARE SO MANY COACHES STRUGGLING TO GET BY?

Whether you are already a coach or are just beginning, you are blessed to be involved in such a wonderful profession. You get to work with dynamic, already-successful people who want to get better, be more effective, and feel more fulfilled. You choose where you work, when you work, and with whom you work. You have valuable tools and powerful insights that make a difference by helping people: overcome limiting beliefs; change their behaviors to improve results; relate better with others; eliminate distractions that keep them from their goals; get back in touch with their natural inspiration and drive; find clarity about which direction to go; and achieve amazing results that may have seemed impossible when first contemplated.

Most readers already know what coaching is and why it is such a powerful way to get results for our clients. For the purposes of this book, coaching is defined as an efficient, high-impact process that helps already high-performing people improve results in ways that are sustained over time.

Let's review each of the key terms in this definition:

First, coaching is **efficient and high-impact** because you work with clients to get big results through short meetings, usually of no more than 60 minutes per session. During this time, you and your client generate valuable insights, gain clarity, and make decisions to improve performance. Compare this to traditional consulting work, which is much less efficient because it often requires invasive outside teams, a stream of analyses, lengthy reports, and PowerPoint presentations that make recommendations, which the client may or may not accept.

Second, coaching is a **process**. You work with clients over time, constantly setting goals and improving. An effective coaching process begins with where the client wants to go, compares that to where they are, and then moves the client forward towards measurable results. The process repeats again and again, in a cycle of continuous improvement.

Third, coaching works with **high-performing people**. It is not therapy, meant to "fix" a person. Your clients are already highly functioning, successful people. Like any of us, they need support, from time to time, in order to perform better.

Finally, your goal as an Executive Coach is to **improve results in ways that are sustainable over time**. Your clients want some sort of outcome. For instance, in the executive coaching world, clients usually seek improved profits, career success, organizational effectiveness, or career and personal satisfaction. If you aren't helping your clients get results, you aren't doing your job. At the same time, coaching is about helping people improve their own capabilities and effectiveness, so that the results and performance improvements last. To use the timeworn and famous quote, you are teaching people to fish, not feeding them for a day.

Coaching has grown significantly, both in acceptance and in the types of practicing coaches. There are all sorts of coaches: life coaches, business coaches, executive coaches, sales coaches, career coaches, image coaches, and, of course, sports coaches. Some professionals only coach. Others have added coaching to an overall suite of services that could include: management consulting, human resources consulting, psychological assessments, training, accounting services, and general business services.

According to a survey by the Hay Group, an international human-resources consultancy, 25 to 40 percent of *Fortune* 500 companies use executive coaches, and that number is projected to grow. Manchester, Inc., a Jacksonville, Florida, career management consulting firm has reported that about six out of ten organizations currently offer coaching, or other developmental counseling, to their managers and executives.

Coaching used to be a last resort to help struggling employees before terminating them. Now it is a standard career development strategy for executives, up-and-coming managers, and top performers. It is also used to give support to people in high-stress jobs, such as salespeople.

One reason that coaching continues to grow is because, when done well, it gets results. According to the International Coach Federation's Global Coaching Client Study, which interviewed 2,165 coaching clients from 64 countries, the median return on investment in coaching for business purposes is seven times the investment. Individual clients reported a median return on their investment of 3.44 times.

The study showed that the majority of coaching clients reported positive changes in a number of areas including: self-confidence, relationships, communication skills, interpersonal skills, work performance, and work/life balance. 83 percent of individuals reported being very satisfied with their coaching experience, and a remarkable 96 percent said they would repeat their coaching experience given the same circumstances.

Given these results, one would expect that coaches should be making a fortune. Sadly, this is not the case. Many coaches struggle to attract new clients and earn the income they want. I get emails and calls from would-be coaches from all around the world; this is what they've shared with me:

- Getting new clients is a constant battle and takes away from my love of coaching.

- Promoting my coaching services feels demeaning and uncomfortable.

- The market seems to be filled with too many coaches, and I don't know how to stand out.

- Nothing is more frustrating than watching less competent coaches, with fewer credentials, attract more clients, and make more money than I do.

- I don't charge enough, but I feel awkward asking for more.

- My income has hit a plateau, and I worry that it is always going to be limited, because there is only so much time in the day to get paid for working with clients.

It doesn't have to be this way, and the purpose of this book is to show you how to make the above issues go away forever. I want you to finish this book knowing exactly what it really takes to build a thriving coaching practice—one that can generate $1 million per year for you, or at least a very comfortable living, depending on your goal.

The book shows you the six required steps to make this happen. Once you put these steps to work for you, everything changes:

- Clients come to you in order to learn more about what you do, so you don't have to feel like business development is a battle.

- Promoting your coaching services and developing business feels natural, not awkward.

- You set yourself apart from the pack, and enjoy the status of being a go-to coach in your market.

- You charge what you are worth, and your clients are glad to pay it.

- You develop sources of leverage in your practice, so that your income potential is nearly unlimited.

Here is a summary of the six steps that will get you to this goal:

STEP ONE: LAY A SOLID STRATEGIC FOUNDATION.

Many coaches start promoting their services before they have thought key strategic questions through. By ignoring or avoiding these questions, they fail to set themselves apart when they try to develop business. As a result, prospects don't have a compelling reason to hire them, and they lose business to coaches who have a clear strategy. A good strategic foundation includes a profitable target market that you can dominate; an understanding of the market's needs; a solution that gets clear results and provides great value; and a marketing message that will compel them to contact you.

STEP TWO: USE LOW-COST, HIGH-IMPACT TACTICS TO GET CLIENTS.

You don't have to spend a fortune on marketing your services to be a very successful coach. However, you must put into place proven approaches to filling your practice with clients. These tactics start with referrals and include: achieving expert status through information and education; online marketing tactics; alliances that bring a stream of clients; leadership in relevant associations and organizations; and a variety of creative strategies to reach top decision makers. The good news is that you can choose the tactics that work best for you, your talents, and your style; there are no one-size-fits-all approaches that you must follow.

STEP THREE: CLOSE ENGAGEMENTS.

Some coaches get everything right when it comes to their strategic foundation and their approach to get visible, but they just can't seem to close a deal and get paid to coach people at the price they want. Closing engagements requires the ability to engage prospects authentically; have open and honest conversations with prospects, to figure out whether there is a good fit or not; develop a solution that works for both parties; handle any objections with finesse and grace; and explicitly ask for a decision. Once you know how to close engagements, business development becomes easier, more natural, and even fun.

STEP FOUR: KEEP CLIENTS FOR LIFE, OR AT LEAST FOR A LONG TIME.

The best source of revenue is almost always current clients. The most successful coaches understand the value of the first client, and every client that follows. They understand what it means to deliver value and create raving fans. Finally, they are diligent when it comes to anticipating client needs and finding new ways to serve them, as well as other people in their organization, professional network, or life.

STEP FIVE: BUILD A FIRM TO ENJOY LASTING WEALTH.

To create a breakthrough coaching firm, you need to think like a firm builder, not like a solo coach. Once you do that, you stop trading your time with clients for dollars, and you instead focus on building a company that is worth something—something that makes money for you while you do other things. This process starts when you develop proprietary methodologies and valuable intellectual property. Once you do, you can turn it into a portfolio of programs and products that you can offer the market. Examples include books and information products, as well as tools to help your clients assess and improve their situation, certifications, and licensing arrangements. You can also contract with other coaches and experts to create larger teams that get bigger engagements, so that others do part or all of the work, while you make more money. Meanwhile, all of this work continues to set you apart as the go-to coaching professional in your market, and allows you to charge even more money for your time.

STEP SIX: CREATE YOUR MILLION-DOLLAR BUSINESS PLAN.

None of the first five steps matter if you don't make a plan and commit to taking action to make it happen.

There are two assumptions that I need to make as you go through the book. If these assumptions are not true for you, the above steps will not work.

First, I assume that you are good at coaching clients to achieve significant results and see value in your services. This is a book about how to market your coaching services; it is not about how to be a good coach. If you are already coaching clients and not getting repeat engagements, a stream of referrals, and generally rave reviews, consider the possibility that you might need additional training in best-practice coaching skills. Even if you have completed one of the better-known coach training programs; even if you have paid top dollar to be trained at a brand-name university, you still might need to strengthen your skills. Many coach training programs are either too academic or too superficial, and don't give you the tools and skills you really need to be successful in the market.

Second, I assume that you are willing to make marketing and firm development a top priority. You can't sit behind a desk waiting for the phone to ring. Hope and prayer are not viable business development strategies for coaches. If you aren't willing to make a significant commitment to marketing, you will not attract clients or earn the income you want and deserve. The fast food industry tells its workers, "If you have time to lean, you have time to clean." In the coaching business, that advice might be restated as, "If you have time to lean, you have time to market your services." This book will show you the most efficient and effective path to success, but knowing how is not the same as getting out there and taking action.

If these assumptions are true for you, then you are ready to build a million-dollar coaching firm. Let's get started!

Step I

LAY A SOLID STRATEGIC FOUNDATION

Many coaches start promoting their services before they have really thought through key strategic questions. By ignoring or avoiding these questions, they fail to set themselves apart when they try to develop business. As a result, prospects don't have a compelling reason to hire them, and they lose business to coaches who do have a clear strategy. A good strategic foundation includes: a profitable target market that you can dominate; an understanding of the market's needs; a solution that gets clear results and provides great value; and a marketing message that compels them to contact you.

Chapter One

THE OPPORTUNITY IS GREATEST WHEN YOU THINK OF YOURSELF AS MORE THAN A COACH

Before marketing your coaching practice, the first question you must answer is, "Why would anyone hire a coach?"

The easy answer is that human resource professionals in many organizations—including *Fortune 500* companies, governments, foundations wanting to build organizational capacity in the non-profits that they fund, and numerous progressive companies—have discovered the value of coaching. They seek out and hire coaches to develop both current and emerging leaders.

However, if your answer stops there, you limit yourself to competing in a relatively small and highly competitive market. You can make a great living if you have a name like Marshall Goldsmith or John Maxwell; if you are affiliated with a top-tier consulting firm like McKinsey; or if you are part of the leadership development group of one of the few huge, well-regarded executive recruiting firms. If you don't have that kind of name recognition or marketing clout, you might find yourself struggling in this market. To get work, you must compete against the thousands of other coaches out there, all of whom are struggling to get approved by one HR department, and then another, and then another. A second option is that you contract with firms that already have large coaching contracts. In this situation you don't own the client relationship, and you have to accept the often stringent hours and terms that the primary contractor demands from you.

Whichever option you choose, you become a commodity, stuck in the trap of accepting an hourly rate in exchange for a set number of coaching hours. Even worse, when you do get clients through this system, you often find that—despite what the HR department or the primary contractor might tell you—your direct coaching clients aren't especially happy to have you as a coach.

To break out of this trap, you have to generate a deeper answer to why anyone would hire a coach. Unfortunately, this answer might be painful for many traditional coaches to swallow.

If we are honest, the vast majority of people don't want to hire a coach at all, and, despite research to the contrary, they don't believe that coaching adds any value. In my own experience, I have found that eighteen out of twenty executives don't want anything to do with coaching. When I first bring it up, they roll their eyes when they hear the word *coach,* and—as one executive shared with me outright—think to themselves, "Coaching is an incredibly expensive waste of time and most coaches are lightweights on the periphery of what matters."

Meanwhile, the eighteenth executive wants a coach, but not for himself. He thinks he is fine the way he is, and wants a coach for the people who really need fixing, namely his management team. Of course, the management team doesn't want to be coached because they think their boss is the problem!

Maybe the twentieth executive I approach about coaching is at least open to the idea. They might be willing to test you out and see if you are useful. Colleagues who do other types of coaching, like small business coaching and life coaching, share the same frustration: It is hard to find people who want to be coached!

The way around this problem is to accept the truth and then come up with another way. Here is a way to reframe this situation that has made all the difference to me and to other successful coaches: People might not want a coach, but they will hire a credible expert who understands their most pressing problems and can help to solve them.

The implications of this shift are profound. It means that we don't try to push coaching onto people. We are not door-to-door evangelists spreading the good news of coaching to an unreceptive audience. Rather, we listen closely to the problems our potential clients face. Then we show that we have an efficient and effective path to help them move forward and get results. We demonstrate that we have the tools and processes to help them reach their most ambitious and exciting aspirations, and to overcome the obstacles that they face today. We prove that we get results based on our knowledge and experience, and that these results provide great value. In other words, we approach our work as solution providers first, and as coaches second.

In this new paradigm, coaching becomes just one of the many ways in which we can deliver results, the same way that a pill is one of many possible ways to deliver medicine to a patient. Think of your knowledge, expertise, and solutions as the medicine. Coaching is just one way to get that medicine to your clients so that they get better. There are other ways to provide that same expertise to clients, and sometimes these are a better fit. That's why many coaches wear multiple hats, including consultant, trainer, mentor, writer, speaker, facilitator, and even interim executive. By the way, wearing multiple hats for clients is a great way to become their trusted advisor.

Think BIGGER than being just a coach!

Coach ➡ Credible Expert
Solution Provider
Thought Leader
Firm Builder

Do you see the difference, and the benefits, that this approach offers you? The first benefit of this approach is that you have an easier time converting prospects to clients. By focusing on their problems and a solution that gets results, instead of on coaching, people are much more receptive to the idea of hiring you. Again, people might not want a coach, but they will hire a credible expert who understands their problems and can help solve them.

Second, this perspective makes it easier for you to become a recognized expert in your target market, the go-to professional that people seek out first. That way, you cut through the clutter in the market and have potential clients come directly to you. You don't have to feel like you are constantly chasing after new clients, especially when you implement the business development strategies described in Step Two of this book.

Perhaps, best of all, when you see yourself in this new light, you can build a firm that generates wealth for you. That's because—like a true expert and thought leader—you can develop methodologies for getting consistent results for each and every client. These methodologies set you apart and also become valuable intellectual capital. Once you have just one methodology in place, you can turn it into all sorts of products and services that earn money for you while you do other things. You can: write books and develop information products, create proprietary assessments, build an online subscription-based website, develop games and simulations, certify others to use your materials with their clients, license your content to other people and companies, and hire other professionals as employees or contractors and have them do the direct client work. Over time, you can also offer related professional services—like executive recruiting and outsourced training programs—to your clients. Really, the sky is the limit, and Step Five of this book will show you how to do these things.

Take a few moments to consider this bigger perspective. What becomes possible for you in your professional practice when you think of yourself as more than a coach? What might change in the way that you market yourself? What new products and services might you offer? How might you create a professional services firm, instead of a solo coaching practice, which generates income for you, and that is a valuable asset should you ever want to sell it?

I sincerely hope that your answers to these questions open up exciting new possibilities for you as a coach—and, of course, as someone who is more than a coach.

Chapter Two

THE THREE REQUIREMENTS FOR ONGOING SUCCESS AS A COACH

ucceeding as a coach is not complicated. There are three requirements. If you do these things well, you will succeed as a coach, as well as positioning yourself as a credible expert, trusted advisor, and solution provider. This chapter describes these three requirements, and each one is woven into the fabric of every single chapter that follows.

To make it easy to remember these three requirements, think of them as the three Rs—except this time R does not stand for reading, writing, and 'rithmetic. For coaches, the three Rs are:

Get Valuable **R**esults;

Build Relevant **R**elationships; and

Keep **R**aising the bar.

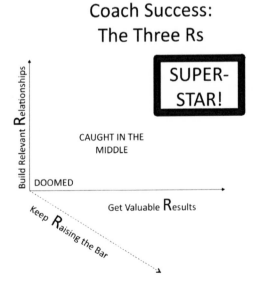

Coach Success:
The Three Rs

As the above graphic shows, if you do these three things consistently and well, you will build a thriving coaching practice and be a coaching superstar. If you don't, you will be doomed and eventually give up in frustration; or you will be caught in the middle and just get by. It's as simple as that.

Let's look at each of the three Rs in turn.

GET VALUABLE RESULTS.

If you don't get meaningful results for your clients, you are not going to have any clients. Specifically, your clients should feel like they are getting results that are worth five to ten times your fees. That way, there is no question about the return on the investment they are getting from your services, and your value is clear.

Results start by understanding your client's most pressing problems. Your client is at point A, and wants to get to the better point B. Maybe he wants to: make more money, get healthier, have better relationships, see his company's sales and profits grow, reduce employee turnover, resolve a conflict with a colleague, or eliminate a behavior that is derailing his career. I won't take an engagement unless the client agrees, up front, that getting to point B is worth five to ten times my fees.

Once you and the client agree that there is great value in solving their problem and bridging the gap, it is time to realize that value and get results. To do this, you and the client need to understand what is causing the gap between point A and point B, and develop an efficient pathway for your client to bridge the gap. This is a crucial coaching skill, and one which many coaches need to improve. Some coaches believe that if they just ask enough open-ended questions, the client will magically have an epiphany and be able to solve the problem on their own. Unfortunately, their questions are sometimes on the periphery of the issue, and don't move the client forward. They don't have voltage. They lack power. The fact is that most clients will not suffer through a list of non-compelling and open-ended questions for long if they don't see progress. One of the reasons why some coaches have a bad reputation in the industry is that they ask lightweight and lazy questions that frustrate the client and fail to lead to insights for better performance.

The solution is to come up with a framework that attempts to explain the gap your client is facing. Then, once you have that framework in place, you can ask targeted, powerful questions, and share valuable insights, that move your client forward. For instance, author Patrick Lencioni has a gift for developing simple, elegant frameworks that address the specific problems that executives and organizations face. In his book *The Five Dysfunctions of a Team*, he presents five core reasons why teams do not perform up to their capacity, and what the team leader has to do to overcome these issues. The reasons include: inattention to results, lack of commitment, and absence of trust. For each issue, he provides a clear action step that the leader needs to take. With a framework like this in place, it becomes easy for him—along with his team, and his affiliates—to coach managers about why their teams are not performing, and what they need to do to improve. He doesn't have to fumble around hoping that he stumbles on the right question or that his client randomly has an insight. Browse the list of best-selling business books and authors—Covey, Blanchard, Senge, Maxwell, Gittomer, Gladwell, Buckingham—and you will discover that most of the authors of these books also have the gift of creating elegant, powerful frameworks that help people have insights and improve. A coach needs to have the same ability, whether they create their own frameworks or use other experts' frameworks—while giving credit and following copyright laws, of course.

Sometimes, when a client presents a new problem, you have to develop this framework on the spot, and be agile. You have to come up with powerful questions that drive your client toward insights and then, if appropriate and with permission, share your own insights. Ideally, your expertise, previous experience, and ability to think on your feet will give you the ability to do this. Over time, if you have a focused target market and set of problems to address, you will likely see the same problems come up over and over again. As you work with more clients, you will identify the range of issues that cause these problems, and create a list of ideas to solve them. Because of this, you can develop your own framework, just like the best-known business experts do, before you meet with your clients. You can also develop a process—which includes a timeline and coaching plan, including how to track results—that serves as a guide to get results. That way, you are prepared going in, and have an efficient, powerful pathway to improved performance.

Once you have a framework and a process in place, you can really set yourself apart. A framework explains the problem and its solutions. A process explains how to move forward to achieve results. Combine the two—the what with the how—and you have a proprietary methodology, which you can brand and call your own. Now you are really in business! People want to hire a professional who has a proprietary methodology, proven to get results and deliver value.

At the same time, you can take your methodology and turn it into a range of programs and services that add value, and bring results to the people in your market: books, information products, assessments, group coaching, training programs, leadership circles, consulting, online subscriptions, certifications, licensing of content to other coaches, and more. Now you can reach a much broader audience, because each program has a different price point. People can choose, based on their budget and perception of your value in relation to the results they expect, how much they pay for access to your expertise.

Even if you don't take your practice to the point where you are offering a variety of services and products, you still need to deliver results. You absolutely need to know how to get your clients from where they are now to the compelling place they want to be, in a way that justifies your fees.

BUILD RELEVANT RELATIONSHIPS.

Many coaches who get great results are frustrated, because they see less competent coaches getting better engagements and making more money. Life is not fair, and the most qualified coach doesn't always get the job. The reason is simple: relationships.

Even if you have a coaching process that transforms lives forever and changes the world, it means nothing if people don't know who you are, and what you can do. That's why the most successful coaches not only spike in their ability to get results, but also in having relevant relationships with the people who make decisions in their marketplace.

There are many types of people, which every coach needs to know in their target market: potential clients; people who can make introductions to potential clients; complementary professionals who serve the same market; thought leaders in the market who can spread the word about us; and people who can provide opportunities to get visible through speaking, writing, and publicity.

Relationships are the currency of your professional practice. Ford Harding, author of *Creating Rainmakers*, makes the observation that the value of your network compounds as it grows, exactly the way that an investment portfolio does. For instance, if you have ten people in your network and add one more person to it, your network doesn't increase in value by just ten percent. It increases by much more, because the new person in your network allows you to make exponentially more connections—with the people in their network, and with the people in your network.

Building business relationships goes hand in hand with getting results and providing value. If you want to strengthen and expand your network, be a giver. Before expecting anything in return, give value first. Learn what the people in your network are trying to achieve, and help them get there. Have explicit conversations about how you can help them, and do your best to make a difference for them. Meanwhile, educate your contacts about the types of introductions and referrals you seek. You don't always get back value equal to what you put in, and so it makes sense to periodically assess your portfolio of relationships, and do some rebalancing if need be. However, if you keep giving first, you will see a strong return over time.

Get visible in front of the people in your target market who you don't know but should. Show them that you are a credible expert and thought leader with solutions to their most challenging problems. Speak. Write. Get active on social media. Do occasional research projects or surveys and publicize them to your market—and include target prospects as participants in your research. Take leadership roles in the community and in associations where decision makers in your target market get together. Get to know people who know them, and build up enough trust to ask for an introduction. It takes time to build credibility and show value to people you don't know, and you really have to make the effort. When you do, you will be pleasantly surprised about the caliber of people you attract to your network.

There is no reason why you can't be one call away from the most important people in your target market: CEOs, entrepreneurs, financiers, recruiters, top vendors, business reporters, consultants, busy coaches who might refer work your way, and leaders in key associations. All it takes is a commitment to building relevant relationships and continuing to strengthen them by helping the people in your network succeed.

KEEP RAISING THE BAR.

The third requirement is to keep building on your success in getting valuable results and building relevant relationships. Coaches cannot sit back on their laurels and expect the phone to keep ringing.

Have you noticed that the luminaries in our field, as well as business gurus in general, keep developing new content? We put out new books, offer new speeches, develop new seminars, and market new coaching programs. The world keeps changing, and so do the problems that our clients face. To remain relevant, you have to keep up with these problems and prepare ways to help people deal with them.

At the same time, people come and go in our target market. Seasoned decision makers and thought leaders retire or decide to do other things. Ambitious up-and-comers become part of the new generation of high-powered people. We have to continue to build our network and keep it current. We have to stay visible to the people in our market by continuing to speak, write, and stay active in social media.

You can't sit still! If you don't constantly raise the bar, your competitors will, and your practice will stagnate.

Take a moment and assess your current practice as a coach. How do you rate yourself on the three Rs? What is one thing you can do, right now, to move towards Superstar status? How can you get better results for your clients, and develop proprietary methodologies that can set you up to be even more dominant in your market? How can you be closer to the key people you need to know and, more importantly, to the people who need to know you? What is one way that you can raise the bar and stay ahead of the competition by providing more significant value and having a stronger network?

Chapter Three

CHOOSE A PROFITABLE TARGET MARKET

A re you ready to get practical? The last two chapters set the stage for success. Now it is time to make some decisions and take specific actions to build a solid strategic foundation—a foundation that will help position your coaching practice to stand apart from the rest.

The place to start is by attacking a profitable target market, one where you can establish yourself as the go-to coaching professional. Many coaches resist this. They think that everyone is a potential client and refuse to make choices. This is a big mistake. I know this to be true, because I made this mistake when I first started out, and my mistake was almost fatal.

When I first tried to build my coaching practice, I thought everyone and anyone in business could be a client. Why not? I had an MBA from a top school, had some significant business experience in multiple industries, and arrogantly figured that I was smart enough to handle any issue that came my way.

Unfortunately, the market did not agree with me. I talked to everyone I knew to find work, and came up empty. Finally, the truth hit me like a pile of bricks. I was sitting with a woman who had been referred to me. I was talking about how I can help people, and she interrupted me, "Andrew, I get that you are smart. But I have no idea what you do as a coach, and I have no idea how to tell others about you. I want to help you, but I'm afraid I don't know how."

That advice floored me. I suddenly realized that if I wanted to succeed as a coach, I needed to focus. Right there and then I decided to go after a target market I knew well: non-profits. I reached out to a local non-profit support association, and offered to do a free seminar for their members on strategic planning for non-profit executives. The head of the association accepted my offer, and marketed the event to members. Twenty-five executive directors came, and I left that meeting with five prospects and two clients. A year later, when I had a thriving practice, I could trace almost all of my clients back to that one seminar.

Since then, if I wanted to go into a new market, I did it strategically. I understand the needs of the market, develop specific solutions, craft messages that speak in language used by the people in the target market, test and refine my ideas by talking to some people in the market, and then find ways to get visible to the key decision makers in that market. Sometimes my efforts pay off, and sometimes they don't. However, when I fail, the act of being visible usually leads me to new contacts who do want my services, and thus to unanticipated new markets. For instance, at one point in my practice, I went after the largest technology companies in Silicon Valley. I made some headway getting to middle managers, but never broke through to the executive suites. However, by speaking, writing, and reaching out to my network, I attracted a lucrative client base of entrepreneurs in small and emerging technology firms.

At the same time, new markets opened up for me through existing ones. For instance, I worked with a non-profit association that had received a grant from the National Science Foundation. That work introduced me to some university administrators who hired me, and from there I was able to create specific coaching solutions for the secondary education market.

Based on this experience, and similar experience shared by other successful coaches, I strongly recommend that you spend at least 70 percent of your time focusing on a target market that you can dominate as the go-to coaching professional. The reasons are compelling and clear:

- The people in the market generally read the same things, go to the same association meetings, and visit the same websites, so you can reach them more easily than if you don't specialize.

- People in the same market know each other and recommend vendors and professionals to one another, which makes it easier for word about your services to spread.

- You can charge higher fees, because your solutions are targeted precisely to their needs.

- You beat out generalists, who lack the depth that people in your target market demand, and who fail to speak the same language as the people in your market.

- You might have a smaller overall market than if you were a generalist, but you convert a much higher percentage of prospects to clients thanks to your specialization, so you make more money.

Many coaches resist the idea of specializing. I used to try to argue with these folks, but I gave up when one reluctant coach said, "I have shiny object syndrome, and there is nothing either you or I can do about it." Now, instead of fighting, I simply suggest that you spend only 70 percent of your time focusing on a target market. Leave 30 percent of your time and effort for clients you can attract through your network or in the course of going after work in your primary market. Sometimes we find success when we aren't looking for it. By leaving 30 percent of your time and effort open to what you attract, you might find the target market that was meant for you in the first place.

There are different types of target markets to choose among:

- *Industry.* Focus on an industry like banking, healthcare, education, or any of the hundreds of other industries. To be even more focused, drill down into the industry. For instance, healthcare includes insurers, providers, and life sciences. Within providers, there are huge health systems, academic medical centers, teaching hospitals, community hospitals, Veterans Administration hospitals, rural hospitals, and various sizes and shapes of physician practices.

- *Function or Job Title.* Specific functions include, among others, CEOs, Chief Financial Officers, Vice Presidents of Human Resources, Chief Technology Officers, Directors of Marketing, Directors of Sales, and Chief Learning Officers. Your target market can be even more powerful by combining function and industry.

- *Demographic Group.* Demographic groups include baby boomers and other specific generations, women, men, and specific ethnic groups. For instance, I know many coaches who specialize in helping women who are fed up with the corporate glass ceiling and leave to start their own firm. As with function, you can get even more focused by combining demographics with industry, for instance, by specializing in female partners and senior associates in major law firms.

- *Groups with Shared Values and Interests.* Many people are in communities that share similar hobbies, values, life experiences, and passions. If you can reach these people easily, you can coach them. Examples include: Christian business owners, socially conscious retirees who want to get back into the workforce, Ivy League graduates, former Peace Corps volunteers, and retired military personnel.

- *Geographic Area.* You can also choose to be the go-to coach in your geographic region. However, if you do, I strongly advise that you combine geography with one of the other target markets. Otherwise, you are still a generalist, and more focused coaches can beat you out.

- *Solution to a Specific Problem.* You can create a coaching practice based on solving a specific problem, especially if it is one that people in one of the above markets face. For instance, you can be the influence coach for healthcare executives, the negotiation coach for purchasing managers, the sales coach for lawyers, or the strategy coach for family-owned businesses. Once you become established as the go-to coach for the problem you solve in one market, you can expand into a related market, and continue to grow from there.

So, how do you choose a target market that's worthy of 70 percent of your time? Following are questions to answer as you weigh your options:

1. *Do you have a compelling story to tell?* Sometimes the best target market is staring you right in the face. It's based on where you are and where you have been. If you were a successful Chief Technology Officer, why not coach up-and-coming technology executives? If you are an expert in international protocol, you can coach expatriates on how to get ahead in their new country. If you have started and sold businesses in the telecommunications industry, then coach entrepreneurs in the same market. If you are a great public speaker, coach people who fear public speaking more than death to be more confident and polished on the stage.

2. *Can you easily reach the people in the market?* One key reason to choose a target market at all is that you can reach people more easily. If your target market is fragmented, you might be better off choosing a different one. For instance, there are twenty million solopreneurs in the United States alone, and yet these people tend to not join groups; I know from experience that it can be challenging to reach them.

3. *Can you address the market's most compelling problems?* You are not going to get hired unless you solve problems and get valuable results for your target market. Make sure that you have a clear understanding of the top issues that keep the people in your market up at night, and that you have a coaching methodology that solves them.

4. *Can the people in the market pay?* If the people in your target market are struggling to get by, it is unlikely that they will free up money to pay for your services. For instance, I know a coach who is passionate about working with elite athletes from the inner city. However, he has had no luck getting people to pay him for his services. Unfortunately, he has a hobby and not a coaching business, and—unless he wants to set up a non-profit and get grants—he needs to find a market that can afford his services.

5. *Will the people in the market pay, even if they see value and have the money?* In some markets, the people face big problems that you can solve, but that doesn't mean that your prospects are willing to part with their money. For instance, many of my colleagues report that physicians have many frustrations in today's world of managed care, and are not particularly happy running their medical practices. Despite what seems like a clear opportunity for a coaching practice, these same colleagues have found very few physicians who are willing to pay an outsider, no matter how qualified they are, to help them be more fulfilled and successful. That's not to say you will have the same experience, and it could be that my colleagues have not come up with the right solution for the physician market. Regardless, if you are going to target a market, make sure that—no matter how wealthy the people in it seem to be— they are willing to pay.

6. *Is the market the right size?* Before you target a market, do some calculations to confirm that you can make a living even if only a tiny fraction of the organizations or clients in your market become clients. For instance, I worked with a firm that targeted the top 1,000 hospital systems in the nation. That was plenty big enough for them to gross millions of dollars per year in revenues—even if they only worked with about 20 systems at any one time. On the other hand, if your target market appears to be huge—like the 20 million small businesses in

the United States—consider the possibility that you should slice it and focus in on a smaller niche where you can be the dominant go-to expert.

7. *Is the market saturated?* You want some competition in your target market because it proves that there is a market for coaching. However, make sure you don't face a situation where almost every company or person already has a coach. The Fortune 500 market is pretty saturated for coaches, and it is not easy to compete against the name brands in the coaching, consulting, and executive recruiting world. However, there are millions of mid-sized companies that are only now discovering the power of business, executive, and sales coaching.

8. *Can you set yourself apart and dominate?* Why target a market unless you can dominate it? You don't have to emerge as the leader overnight, but at least give yourself a chance. Make sure you can establish credibility, can tell a story about why people should hire you, understand the market's problems and language, and have a solution that brings them unquestioned value.

9. *Do you want to work with the people in this market?* There are many, many lucrative target markets out there. However, if you don't like the people in them, have conflicts with the shared values and ethics that prevail, or fail to find the problems and challenges that people face, then find another market to serve. You won't be successful if you don't have the passion.

It is hard to choose a target market. Nobody wants to feel like they are limiting their options. It is difficult to commit in a world of so many choices. It is even more difficult to follow through and go deep, developing solutions and marketing messages targeted to a niche. There are no guarantees that the market you choose will also choose you, at least not in the beginning. It might take time, finesse, and having to respond to some tough feedback before you develop a winning strategy, and attract clients in your chosen target market. In some cases, you might decide that you made the wrong choice, and have to start from scratch once again. If that does happen, at least you will have a base of knowledge, and will have learned some valuable lessons for when you start again.

But you have to do it. While you might take comfort in having 20 million potential clients, you ultimately get much more business, and make more money, with a focused target market. You have fewer potential clients, but your conversion rate will be much higher so that you get more actual clients. Ultimately you enjoy greater success. Potential clients will see that you are serious and committed, not a dabbler, and they will respond more positively than to generalists.

At the same time, the 70/30 rule gives you the freedom to spend 30 percent of your time and energy as a generalist, open to whatever comes your way. You get the best of both worlds! Also, once you establish a strong presence in one market, you can move on to another, related market.

What will be your target market?

Case Study: Marc Pitman, The Fundraising Coach

Marc Pitman gets it when it comes to choosing a target market and dominating it. Go to his website www.FundraisingCoach.com and you immediately see the benefits of going deep and serving a focused target market. Everything there—his blog, solutions, book, speaking, seminars, and videos—are focused on helping non-profits get better at fundraising, especially the face-to-face ask. Also, his website is a great case study of the right things to do to have a successful online web presence. I particularly appreciate the way that he uses his red bowtie as part of his branding, both in his thumbnail photo and to dot the "i" in *fundraising.*

Marc started his practice in 2003. Coaching had always been important to his life. He and his wife got some formal coaching before getting married. He also had a life coach while working at a boarding school. "I loved having someone outside the system to brainstorm with, someone who couldn't fire me, and who could see the good things in me. I can see the bad things, and need help seeing the good. I fell in love with coaching as a concept."

Three things caused him to choose fundraising as his coaching niche. First, "I always heard that you have to have a niche. Everything in me resists having a niche. I want to have a bigger platform, and help more people. Common sense says that I should be all things to all people. But I've studied successful people and they all say the same thing: Choose a niche."

Second, he has met coaches who don't have a niche, and he doesn't like the way they come across. For instance, "Someone came up to me the other day and said, 'I'm a dream coach.' She had all this energy and enthusiasm and weirdness. She couldn't explain it beyond that, despite my asking. 'I work with people's dreams!' Dreams could mean something you dreamed the night before, or it could mean what you want to be in life. It was chilling to me, and a horrible way to market coaching services. In my own case, I always did goal setting and time management, and thought about those as my niche, but those are almost as amorphous as being a dream coach. I had been doing fundraising since the mid-1990s. That was a focused niche."

Third, he was on a free teleseminar about coaching, and the speaker was talking about how you have to choose a niche. Marc did a Google search for "Fundraising Coach" during the seminar, and nothing came up. Before the call was over, he'd registered the domain name: www.FundraisingCoach.com. During the call, he noticed that the other people on the call weren't hearing the advice of the speaker. "Their niches were as soft as marshmallows," he explains.

Marc has even refined his niche further. He can coach people about all sorts of fundraising, but his real sweet spot is asking for money face to face from both existing donors and prospective donors.

When it comes to getting visible, Marc calls himself a "consummate bootstrapper." He explains, "Since I've never had money for advertising, social media and my online presence have been the core of my marketing strategy." He was, and continues to be, an avid student of social marketing. He follows what he admits is a "well-trodden path" with his online marketing: blogging, building his email list, sending out newsletters every other week, and using Facebook, Twitter, and LinkedIn. "I try *not* to be on the cutting edge with social media. I follow the blogs of people who experiment with online marketing. Often they'll say that some new technology is the best thing since sliced bread, and three months later they'll write that they don't use it anymore. I'm a constant student of what works."

His focus on a niche forces him to be disciplined in the keywords he uses online. "I try to be very clear and use SEO-friendly language. For instance, the term 'fundraising ideas' gets searched 10,000 times per month. But people who search that term could be looking for popcorn and cookie sales at a local school fundraiser. Fewer people search for words like *fundraising training, fundraising book, fundraising speaker,* and *fundraising coaching,* but these people are better fits for my services."

Similarly, he writes a lot about Twitter and fundraising, even though he isn't sure that Twitter is a productive fundraising device. "It brings people to the site. Twitter is consistently in the top five or six search terms for people finding my site. It starts the initial conversation."

Marc also does a lot of public speaking. He started speaking at conferences for free, always collecting business cards from participants. He asks participants to write a dollar sign on their card if they want to be added to his newsletter list. Gradually he asked for his expenses to be reimbursed for his speeches, and now he charges stipends when he speaks. "*Stipend* and *honorarium* are nice words, less brash than *money* or *fee.*"

Having a book has been, in his words, "amazing" for his credibility. He shares, "Credibility is a fickle thing. With a book, even though I haven't changed what I'm doing or who I am, now I'm an author. I've done eBooks and blogs, but having a tangible book that doesn't look self-published has really built my credibility. Recently I was in New York, to be interviewed on a show. The producer came out and held up my book. It's intentionally a slim, non-intimidating book for board members. I was going to be interviewed about something only tangentially related to fundraising, but the producer hefted the book and said, 'Okay, you're legit...'"

Mark also does cold calling, but less for results than for getting into the right mindset. "Cold calling doesn't bring me much business. But when I do them, people come to me out of the blue. When you tend one field, the harvest might come from another place. It feels serendipitous. When I don't do cold calling, the calls don't come. It puts me in the right mindset, maybe a sales mindset, and things happen when I do it."

Marc's aspiration is less about hiring coaches than creating products. "Part of me would love to have a cohort of coaches, but I like being solo." He offers a paid newsletter for a monthly fee, which generates extra income while also keeping him disciplined about creating content; it also generates new clients for him. He also serves as one of a number of non-profit gurus in a membership community for non-profit executives and boards. Finally, he continues to write books, too, while considering the idea of creating a certification program for non-profit coaches.

As a result of his focus and smart marketing strategies, Marc has become a dominant presence in the non-profit niche. "Once you start showing up at professional associations and magazines catering to your niche, you gain a certain image that sets you apart."

Chapter Four

UNDERSTAND THE NEEDS IN YOUR MARKET

've never met a coach who wasn't passionate about human potential, leadership development, and all sorts of powerful ways to help people become more self-aware, overcome limiting beliefs, create more effective habits, and achieve breakthrough results. However, this passion can get in the way of attracting clients. Sometimes coaches push their passion so hard that prospects recoil, and run in the opposite direction.

In other words, it is rare for someone to wake up and say to themselves, "I have reached the conclusion that I need to transform my beliefs, find distinctions that help me be more effective, complete a personality inventory assessment, and figure out what my behavioral blind spots are. I'd better hire a coach." Similarly, if you corner a potential client and start talking about these things with them and how exciting they are, you will see them checking their watches and trying to find the nearest escape route.

If you want to attract new clients, you have to get into the prospect's head and understand their way of seeing things. You have to tap into their aspirations and perceived needs first, so that you can show that you have a solution that is valuable to them. As one of my mentors taught me, "Listen to the messages your prospects are sending to you, and then answer the mail."

For instance, one of my markets for coaching is non-profits. Non-profit executive directors and board members are wonderful to work with, because they are generally open to coaching. Also, they often have an interest in psychology and personal development, and so they understand what coaching is all about. However, I don't market coaching engagements to them by starting off with a discussion of coaching and why I think coaching is so great.

Instead, I attract clients in this market by focusing in on their top needs. This includes:

- Getting the board of directors to come together and agree on a strategic direction;

- Having the board be more active in fund raising;

- Avoiding the burnout that is so common among executive directors in the non-profit world;

- Developing front-line managers and getting them to think about the bigger picture.

Once I engage with an executive director on the above issues—whether on my website, blog posts, or in one-on-one conversations—it becomes much easier to get hired. They see that I understand their needs. From there, it is a natural transition to talk about solutions, including a coaching process.

Similarly, when I target executives in large health systems, I don't start out by suggesting that they might benefit from having a coach. Instead, I focus in on their unique pain points, including:

- Struggling to remain profitable despite managed care and constant changes in government reimbursement rules;

- Coping with the costs of providing free care to indigent populations;

- Recruiting and retaining top nursing talent during a historic nursing shortage;

- Developing nursing managers to step up from front-line patient care and lead the organization forward;

- Getting physicians on board with the need to reduce utilization of supplies and discharge patients to less acute care;

- Competing against more agile, standalone surgery centers, diagnostic facilities, and labs; and

- Improving labor productivity across units and ancillary departments.

For any market that I serve as a coach, I've done my homework. I know what the key problems are. I learn how to phrase them in their language, and use their buzzwords instead of coaching buzzwords. My marketing materials, including my website, articles I write, speeches I give, and blogs I post all begin with a discussion of the problems that cause pain for the people in my target market. Similarly, if a potential client wants to talk more about what I do, I start any conversation with a prospect by focusing on their perceived issues by asking pointed questions to understand their compelling problems.

How about you?

Now that you have chosen a target market, it is time to really understand the problems the people in that market face. Go as deep as you can, starting with your own experience and knowledge. Contact industry associations. Read every relevant publication about your target market. You might even do a research study and interview a sample of people in your market. Ask them what their top concerns and challenges are. What are these problems costing them and their organizations? What is the emotional toll of these issues on the various stakeholders involved? How have they been addressing them? What has worked and what hasn't? What will happen if these problems continue?

You know you are onto something when you discover a problem that has both intellectual consequences and emotional distress. In the executive and business coaching world, intellectual consequences can include: lost sales and profit, lower productivity, poor morale, high employee turnover, quality issues, lack of time, constant firefighting, losing market share, resistance to change, and unclear communication. Emotional distress might include: fear, stagnation, anger, dismay, unnecessary struggle and hassle, embarrassment, loss of control, anger, and even disgust.

Once you know the problems that your market faces, good things will start to happen. First, you can craft a compelling marketing message that gets attention and response. Which of the following two marketing messages would you respond to if you were a university administrator?

MESSAGE A:

Stop struggling to commercialize your university's research and earn lucrative royalty deals. Read more to discover a high-impact process that will bring new revenue streams to your university....

MESSAGE B:

I am a credentialed coach who specializes in working with university administrators. Read more about my coaching services and me....

Message A taps into the emotional pain that many university administrators feel. It is about them, and touches on their problems and aspirations. Message B is almost all about the coach. Focus first on your niche's top problem. That way, you have a better chance of capturing interest and persuading potential clients to learn more.

The second benefit of starting with your market's problems is that you will have an easier time turning prospects into clients when you meet with them. They want to talk about their issues and concerns first, not about your passion for coaching and all that you claim it can do. Once you discover their biggest problems and what they are costing, you can more easily make the case that your fees are well worth the investment.

Third, to succeed as a coach, you need to develop coaching methodologies that specifically solve your target market's biggest problems and bring value to them. To become a client, someone needs to know that you have a proven, effective, efficient path to results and to solving their most difficult challenges. Once you understand your market's top issues, you can develop the targeted coaching solutions that people want. The next chapter shows you just how to do that.

Chapter Five

DEVELOP ROBUST COACHING SOLUTIONS FOR YOUR MARKET

I f you completed the previous chapter, you should have a good understanding of the most pressing problems the people in your target market face. Now it's time to develop solutions that address these problems, and bring your client value worth five to ten times your fees.

Unfortunately, most coach training programs do not prepare coaches to do this. A robust coaching solution is not a series of weekly meetings where the coach asks open-ended questions in the hopes that the client has a sudden insight and magically knows how to move forward. This is true, even if you start out with an off-the-shelf assessment tool to learn more about the client's personality, leadership style, or communication tendencies. In the coaching big leagues, where clients are paying top dollar and the stakes are high, that's a sure way to get fired quickly.

A robust coaching solution includes five things:

1. A clear understanding of where the client is now and where he wants to be.

2. An elegant, comprehensive framework that allows the coach and the client to assess and then get to the root cause of the gap between where the client is now and where he wants to be.

3. An efficient and effective process that helps the client get where he wants to be. This process includes a proven tool kit made of any or all of the following, depending on the specific situation: relevant assessments, directed coaching conversations, interactive exercises, training, facilitation, mentoring, group work, and assignments that relate directly to success with the specific problem the client faces. It can also include off-the-shelf products and services that you license or

purchase elsewhere, such as psychological inventories, management simulations, team-building tools, and workbooks.

4. A structure that sets goals, tracks goals, and makes mid-course corrections.

5. Follow-up support to make sure that the desired results stick, even after the coaching is done.

For instance, suppose that two coaches are developing a coaching solution to help associates in large consulting firms to feel more comfortable engaging prospects in selling conversations, close more deals, and advance to partnership faster. Each coach has done research showing that this is a big problem in the professional services industry, and they have decided to tackle it.

Following are the solutions that each coach has developed. Guess which coach has the best chance of being successful in the market?

COACH A

Our coaching process starts by setting sales goals with your partners and associates, including a timeline and breaking these goals down into manageable pieces. Then we do a process of inquiry with each associate to understand their perceptions about selling, during which we come up with a custom plan for each individual to achieve his or her goals. Each associate also takes the Myers-Briggs and DiSC assessment to understand his or her natural style. I personally meet one-on-one every week for one hour with each associate, and also have a monthly group coaching session, to assess progress, discuss issues, and develop a plan to overcome them. During this process, which typically lasts six months, we track and celebrate new sales.

COACH B

Many consulting firms report that they are frustrated by the fact that their associates do not generate much or any revenue, which slows the growth of the firm and puts an undue burden on partners. Our extensive research about sales success among professional service firms, as distinguished from other types of businesses, shows that there are five issues that prevent associate-level employees from succeeding in generating six figures or more in consulting revenues:

1. *Negative perceptions about what it means to sell.*

2. *Limiting beliefs about their ability to engage in selling conversations.*

3. *Lack of natural, authentic conversations that make it easy to assess fit with clients and move towards a decision.*

4. *A sink-or-swim culture at many firms that doesn't give associates adequate time to enjoy small initial wins.*

5. *Lack of a common language to describe the consultative sales process.*

Once these issues are removed, associates are capable of generating as much as $1.25 million in revenues by their second year of developing business. Given this framework, our coaching solution first assesses associates on their beliefs and skills in selling situations, using our proprietary consultative selling assessment tool. Based on the results of that assessment, we develop a custom one-on-one coaching plan for each associate. Each plan focuses on the specific development needs of the individual and is designed to build on their strengths, develop new skills, and overcome any limiting perceptions about selling that they may have.

As soon as the assessment phase is complete, we work with partners to set individual sales goals for each associate. We start with small goals for add-on work with existing clients and progress towards small initial sales with new clients, leading to major sales with current and new clients. We track these goals and sales on a report that all associates see; they see where they stand compared to their colleagues, but they only see their name on the report to respect confidentiality.

In addition to one-on-one coaching, participants come to a series of twelve half-day training sessions, on a weekly basis, where we create a common language for sales, role play common selling situations, and videotape associates in action so that they learn by watching themselves on tape.

We work with associates for a full year, making adjustments for each associate depending on their progress and obstacles. We also provide a complimentary follow-up midway through year two to confirm that results have been sustained, and provide up to two months of weekly coaching at no charge if any associates in the program have lost momentum.

In our experience with firms of your size, the average associate can expect to sell as much as $250,000 in the first six months of this process, $750,000 by the end of the first year, and $1.25 million in their second year. Of course, some associates sell *less and some sell more; the process also becomes a data-driven way for partners to identify associates with high potential in the firm.*

I don't know about you, but I'd hire Coach B. In the chart below, notice how Coach B has all of the elements of a solution to one of the problems the target market faces. Coach A's solution includes a few of these elements, but does not appear to be as thorough or as deep as what Coach B proposes, especially in the second and third elements.

Elements of a Robust Solution	Example from Coach B's Solution
1. A clear understanding of where the client is now, and where he wants to be.	Associate-level employees go from generating $0 in year one to $1.25 million by year two.
2. An elegant and comprehensive framework that allows the coach and client to assess and then get to the root cause of the gap between where the client is now, and where he wants to be.	There are five issues that prevent associate-level employees from succeeding in generating six figures or more in consulting revenues: 1. Negative perceptions about what it means to sell; 2. Limiting beliefs about their ability to engage in selling conversations; 3. Lack of natural, authentic conversations that make it easy to assess fit with clients and move towards a decision; 4. A sink-or-swim culture at many firms that doesn't give associates adequate time to enjoy small initial wins, and 5. Lack of a common language to describe the consultative sales process.

3.	An efficient and effective process that helps the client get where he wants to be. This process includes a proven tool kit made of any or all of the following, depending on the specific situation: relevant assessments, directed coaching conversations, interactive exercises, training, facilitation, mentoring, group work, and assignments that relate directly to success with the specific problem the client faces.	Our coaching solution first assesses associates on their beliefs and skills in selling situations, using our proprietary consultative selling assessment tool. Based on the results of that assessment, we develop a custom one-on-one coaching plan for each associate, where we focus on their specific development needs and develop a plan to build their skills and overcome any limiting perceptions. In addition to one-on-one coaching, participants come to a series of twelve weekly half-day training sessions where we create a common language for sales, role play common selling situations, and videotape associates in action so that they learn by watching themselves on tape.
4.	A structure that sets goals, tracks goals, and makes mid-course corrections.	We work with partners to set individuals sales goals for each associate. We start with small goals for add-on work with existing clients and progress towards small initial sales with new clients, leading to major sales with current and new clients. We track these goals and sales on a report that all associates see; they see where they stand compared to their colleagues, but they only see their name on the report to respect confidentiality. We work with associates for a full year, making adjustments for each associate depending on their progress and obstacles.

5.	Follow-up support to make sure that the desired results stick, even after the coaching is done.	We also provide a complimentary follow-up midway through year two to confirm that results have been sustained, and provide up to two months of weekly coaching at no charge if any associates in the program have lost momentum.

It doesn't matter whether you are a life coach, business coach, executive coach, career coach, fitness coach, image coach, meditation coach, hula hoop coach, or any other kind of coach. If you want to earn top dollar and set yourself apart from the crowd, you need to have a solution at least as robust as what Coach B offers to his clients.

One effective way to communicate your solution is with a diagram. A good diagram can convey what you do to get results for clients, and how you do it. For instance, the chart below depicts the hypothetical, high-level methodology of a fitness trainer who specializes in helping affluent weekend warriors get in better shape.

The Total Fitness Weekend Warrior Coaching Method

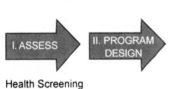

CARDIO COACHING
Running, Jump Rope, Stair Climbs, Cardio Box
Progressive increases in incline/speed

STRENGTH COACHING
Asymmetrical exercises
Unconventional objects
Upper, Lower, Core, Balance/Posture

I. ASSESS

Health Screening
Body Type
Core Strength
Upper Body Strength
Lower Body Strength
Balance and Posture
Cardio Fitness
Flexibility
Current Dietary Plan
Attitudes
Goals

II. PROGRAM DESIGN

SPEED & AGILITY COACHING
Sport-specific
On the actual playing field
Proprietary 4-phase warm up
Chaos drills, resistance running, cone drills

NUTRITIONAL COACHING
Weekly weigh-ins
Calorie manual
Reframing beliefs about food
Recreating meal plan

TRACK, ADJUST ATTITUDE, CELEBRATE!

The graphic shows three phases: assessment, program design, and implementation. This three-phase process is a common model that many successful coaches use. A three-phase process like this is simple; we can all remember three phases. People seem to respond well to a process that starts with an assessment, moves into design, and then gets into implementation. Of course, you can change the names of the phases to suit the needs of your clients and the situation. For instance, my strategic coaching solution also has three phases, but with very different titles. For that process, the three phases are: 1. Answer the big-picture questions. 2. Set priorities, and 3. Implement priorities.

The above fitness coaching solution is more than just a process map. The coach also incorporates his framework about how he helps his clients get better. During the assessment, he looks at eleven elements, including overall health, body type, strength, cardio fitness, flexibility, dietary plan, attitudes, and goals. After he designs a program for his client, his implementation phase includes a variety of different fitness and nutritional coaching approaches, depending on the client's needs. Clients get some form of cardio, strength, speed and agility, and nutritional coaching, depending on his or her individual goals and needs. Finally, the coach tracks the client's goals throughout the program, and helps the client adjust their attitude if they waver, while celebrating their success. This single page allows this fitness coach to set himself apart in a crowded field. Most fitness coaches have some sort of approach inside their heads, but very few actually turn their expertise into an explicit methodology and valuable solution.

Again, every coach needs to develop well-defined solutions to at least one, and ideally a range, of problems that the market faces. These solutions allow you to create repeatable methodologies, while leaving room for you to customize programs to specific client needs. Once you have one or more solutions mapped out, you have an edge over the vast majority of coaches in the market. You also have valuable intellectual capital that you can turn into a range of programs and products, or train and certify others to offer while you earn additional profits.

By this point, you have chosen a target market, you understand the issues the people in your market face, and you have developed solutions to bring valuable results to them. However, none of this matters unless you have crafted a marketing message that attracts interest. The next chapter shows how to do that...

Chapter Six

DEVELOP YOUR COMPELLING MARKETING MESSAGE AND BRAND

A good marketing message for a coach compels prospects to want to learn more about your solutions and how you can help. Unfortunately, many coaches come across as anything but compelling, especially when they describe their services. There are a few reasons why:

1. They don't focus on a target market, and so they come across as yet another generic coach.

2. They talk too much about themselves, and not enough about the prospect.

3. They don't give the prospect reason to keep reading, for instance, by showing a clear understanding of the prospect's top problems and what they are costing or by describing a valuable set of benefits.

4. They fail to engage the prospect emotionally.

5. They don't have an edge that sets them apart from competing coaches, consultants, trainers, and other professionals.

6. They don't provide proof in the form of testimonials and case studies, and so the prospect is unconvinced.

7. There is no call to action, and so the prospect finished reading and doesn't do anything.

A good marketing message is like a good movie—one so good that the viewer won't leave the theatre even if they have to use the bathroom really, really urgently. You want to hook your prospect during the very first scene, and keep him or her riveted throughout.

The way to do this is by using the same tactics used by the best screenwriters. First, the best scripts start with a problem, some sort of tension that captures our interest. Think about your favorite movie. I guarantee you that the main character in that movie faces some sort of big problem or tension, one that gets us engaged straight away. For instance, one of my favorite movies is *The King's Speech*. The main character is a member of the royal family, and is frequently called upon to give speeches. However, he has a serious stuttering problem. Speaking is painful for him, his audience, and for us while we watch him struggle through a speech. As war approaches and he becomes King of England, he has to give the biggest speech of his life. We root for him and, perhaps more, for his unconventional speech therapist as they work together to fix his impediment so he can rally the people of his country.

On the surface, stuttering, the history of early 20th century England, and speech therapy are not particularly glamorous or exciting topics. However, this movie managed to engage and inspire its audience by creating a compelling problem. Then, once hooked, it led us through a journey that resulted in a successful resolution.

Your marketing message needs to do the same thing. You need to capture your audience's attention right away, and compel them to keep reading. People are too busy these days, and too impatient to suffer through a cheesy sales pitch, generic description of your coaching services, or copy that doesn't speak directly to their problems and needs.

As a first step, come up with a one-sentence hook that tells people who you help and how. The template is simple: "I help X to get Y." X is your target market. Y is the most compelling benefit you offer. However, it's phrased in such a way that gets the attention of your target market and has them wanting to learn more.

For instance:

- I help brilliant technology experts become brilliant managers.
- I help healthcare executives make their hospitals more productive while maintaining or improving the quality of patient care.
- I help associates in law firms to become rainmakers.
- I help athletes over 30 to avoid injury.
- I help CEOs who get nervous before major speeches to feel confident and relaxed, connect with their audience, and have the impact they want.

- I help women who feel trapped in the corporate world to break free and start their dream businesses.

- I help managers and executives in financial services prepare for, and succeed in, new roles.

- I help seasoned technology professionals from Eastern Europe to find positions in United States-based technology companies and have successful careers here.

Notice how none of the above messages use the word *coach* or *coaching*. They focus on benefits. They are all designed to have the prospect say, "That's interesting. Tell me more." This single sentence is not a complete marketing message, but it can be an effective tagline for a website, and a great conversation starter at a networking meeting.

Your complete marketing message has the following five elements:

ONE:

Talk about the biggest problem your market faces, and what it is costing them. Do so in a way that makes your reader think, "I have that problem, it is painful, and I'd better keep reading to learn how to solve it."

An effective way to talk about problems is by starting with a verb that captures the pain they are feeling. Examples include:

- Stop struggling with…

- Stop being frustrated by…

- Stop being sick and tired of…

- You don't have to endure the headaches and hassles of…

- Stop putting up with…

From there, you can expand on the problem by talking about what your clients and colleagues in the market tell you it is costing them. What are the top three costs that are really causing them to feel pain, fear, anger, irritation, frustration, and dismay? The more you can tap into these emotions, the more you earn the right to have them keep reading.

For instance:

Non-Profit Executive Directors:

Stop struggling to get your board of directors on the same page about your organization's strategy. Non-profit leaders from all over the country share with me the following frustrations about strategic planning:

- *Nobody on the board even agrees what strategy is, and so the board spends hours and hours debating what strategy should be, without ever doing strategy.*

- *For every board member, it seems like there are at least two ideas about the right strategy, and it feels like herding cats to bring people together.*

- *The board has no process for making decisions about strategy, and so we remain rudderless; this is very uncomfortable and awkward.*

- *Some board members hijack strategic planning meetings, often with frustrating, annoying tangents that don't help move the organization forward and get clarity.*

- *No one on the board feels accountable for making sure the strategy gets implemented, and it is heartbreaking to see the strategy sitting on the shelf gathering dust.*

- *You feel a sense of hopelessness and burnout.*

TWO:

Describe your solution and its benefits in terms that make the hairs on the back of their neck tingle with anticipation.

After you lay out the problem statement, your marketing message should offer a ray of hope. A good transition statement is, "It doesn't have to be this way." Then you can shift to talking about your solution and its benefits. To continue with the non-profit example:

It doesn't have to be this way. My firm has a three-part strategic planning coaching and facilitation process that gets your organization aligned, energized, and moving forward—with a strategy that helps you realize your mission, raise the required funds, and strengthen your reputation in the community. With this process, everything changes:

- *The board has a common language for the strategy and what it means, and is prepared to focus on the strategic questions that have the biggest impact.*

- *Board members have a process to be heard, discuss options, and then make decisions efficiently and effectively, so that it never feels like you are herding cats again.*

- *Your strategic planning meetings are efficient, effective, and well-organized, and board members rave about how well they are run.*

- *The strategy gets implemented, and both you and the board feel a sense of satisfaction and fulfillment to see your organization move forward and focus on serving your constituents and realizing your mission.*

- *You feel recharged in your job, because you know where the organization is headed, know that the board is aligned, and feel empowered to make things happen.*

THREE:

Tell them why you have a unique edge that sets you apart from any other competitor in the market, and makes you the ideal person to solve their problem.

There will always be competition in your market, and you need to know why you are the best solution provider your prospect should hire. You need to know your unique selling proposition, and be able to fill in the sentence, "Unlike others, we…."

Fortunately, there are many types of advantages that are compelling, whether on their own or as part of a larger package:

- A proprietary methodology, as described in the previous chapter. In the coaching world, a proprietary solution is like software or an invention in the technology world. It is a unique solution that you, and only you, own and can deliver. If you can prove that your solution works, you have an instant advantage over coaches who lack such a solution.

- Your unmatched understanding of the market you serve, the problems the people in your market face, and how to solve them. Once again, focusing on a target market gives you an edge!

- Your depth and breadth of expertise, for instance, based on your years of experience, client roster, specific achievements, and talent you can call on through employee and contractor relationships.

- Alliances with other professionals who bring depth, breadth, and their strong reputation to bear on your coaching solutions.

- A unique marketing relationship, such as a relationship with an association where you are a preferred, or even exclusive, provider of coaching services.

- Status as a thought leader in your industry, for instance by being a frequent speaker at association meetings, having a popular blog, writing a book, and in general being visible as someone who is constantly working to provide valuable education and information to your market.

The non-profit coach might describe his edge as follows:

Unlike other advisors, our proprietary strategic planning, coaching, and facilitation process has been designed specifically for non-profit organizations and the unique needs of non-profits. Joe Smith, who is a leading expert on non-profit strategic planning in the world, developed it. His latest book, Herding Cats: A Breakthrough Non-Profit Strategic Planning Process, *is a best seller on* Amazon.com *and has made him a sought-after speaker nationwide. Joe is also on the board of the leading non-profit association in the industry, and has 15 years' experience as the founder and executive director of XYZ for Kids, a successful non-profit in Seattle, Washington. Meanwhile, in addition to Joe, our coaches are former executive directors and board members of non-profits, experience that gives them unmatched insights about what it really takes to develop a strategic plan and implement it.*

The above is only an example and is not meant to overwhelm you or make you think that you'll never be able to compete. Every coach has an edge, even when first starting out. You just need to figure out your unique strengths, and then describe them in a way that matters to the people in your market. You have to claim your power as a coach. If in doubt, start by creating a proprietary solution and branding it with a unique name. This, plus your past experience and focus on a target market, can be more than enough to get you started. As you get more clients, can report more results, add to your solutions, and get more and more well-known in your marketplace as a credible expert, word about you will spread, and your edge will only become more impressive.

FOUR:

Prove it. People are more skeptical than ever before, and it is up to you to prove that everything you have said so far is accurate. Share testimonials, case studies, awards, credentials, client lists, things you have written, things that have been written about you, videos, blogs, and books—anything that proves that you are credible and really do deliver the results you promise.

Even if you are starting out, you can still do most of these things to provide proof. For instance, if you want testimonials, ask your colleagues to write a couple of sentences about your character and intelligence, even if they are not clients. Whenever I want new testimonials, I find a place to speak, and at the end I ask participants to write down the one thing they enjoyed most about the presentation. Then I ask them for permission to use their names on my website. Without specifically asking for a testimonial or even using that word, I can get dozens of testimonials after a single speech!

You can also create proof by being active in your target market as a speaker, blogger, writer, leader and mentor at relevant membership associations as well as someone who is connected on LinkedIn to the movers and shakers in the industry. These are all business development activities, covered in the next part of the book. However, these help you to build your credibility and show your market that you offer valuable solutions.

FIVE:

Have a call to action. You've taken all this time to get your prospect totally engrossed in the problems they are facing, a solution, why you are uniquely qualified to provide that solution, and proof that what you have said is true. It would be a sorry waste if at this point you forget to include a call to action.

Of course, it would be ideal if you could make a call to action that invited your prospect to get started with a coaching program today. However, it is very unlikely that someone will hire you as a coach right after their first look at your website, or an article you have written. I've had some clients do that, but it is a rare occurrence, just as it is rare for someone to get married after one or two dates. Clients, like spouses, typically require a longer courtship.

It is better to be patient and build your credibility over time. Therefore, the best call to action is to offer something low risk, but highly valuable to the prospect. In exchange, the prospect can give you their email address so you can follow up with them over time. Examples include: a free eBook, an invitation to a free webinar, the ability to download a video of one of your speeches, access to a free member area with some valuable resources they can download, or a free assessment. Once you have their contact information, you can follow up with them with even more value and information, until you establish enough credibility for them to be open to a formal coaching arrangement.

Some coaches offer a free coaching session in their call to action, and report that it works well for them. While I encourage you to test this strategy for yourself, it hasn't worked for me. First, I want my clients to have skin in the game, and if I am coaching them for free, they might be more inclined to be a passive observer instead of an active, committed, and engaged participant. Second, many prospects won't take you up on this offer, because—despite the free aspect—you still haven't established enough trust, rapport, and credibility for them to want to invest an hour of their time or open up to you. Third, free coaching sounds a lot like a free consultation, which has the connotation of being a hidden sales pitch. Fourth, I have found that it is hard to convert someone who is getting free coaching into a paying client. Often these people don't have the budget or desire to pay, and I feel like I am wasting my time with most of them.

You can test a variety of different calls to action and see what works best for you, especially in terms of getting contact information so you can follow up with prospects over time. From there, make sure that every single interaction you have with a prospect includes a call to action. Make it a habit. You should have a call to action in every newsletter, speech, webinar, seminar, blog entry, eBook, and even Twitter post. Test out different calls to action, and keep tweaking and improving based on the results you get.

With the above five pieces in place, you should be armed with a powerful marketing message. You can adapt this message to different media, including your website and your firm's bio. Also, use the same template when you give a speech, write an article, or send out a newsletter. However, put more of an emphasis on the audience's problems, offering step-by-step solutions, and proving your solutions through case studies and examples that your solution works. When people expect you to provide information, they want 99 percent content; sales pitches immediately turn them off.

Now that you have your marketing message in your arsenal, it is time to put it to use to attract clients....

Step II

USE LOW-COST, HIGH-IMPACT TACTICS TO GET CLIENTS

You don't have to spend a fortune on marketing your services to be a very successful coach. However, you must put into place proven approaches to filling your practice with clients. These tactics start with referrals and go on to include: achieving expert status through information and education, online marketing tactics, alliances that bring a stream of clients, leadership in relevant associations and organizations, and a variety of creative strategies to reach top decision makers. The good news is that you can choose the tactics that work best for you, your talents, and your style; there are no one-size-fits-all approaches that you must follow. Also, once you get started, each new tactic reinforces the others, and you enjoy an upward spiral of visibility that attracts more and more clients your way.

Chapter Seven

SET UP YOUR TESTING LABORATORY

There are many ways to attract coaching clients, and the most effective ways don't cost much, if any, money. However, you still need to figure out which marketing tactics work best for you, and then continue to improve them over time.

A useful metaphor for this process is the testing laboratory. Whether you are starting out as a coach, or already have a successful practice, you should conduct constant tests about what works and what doesn't to attract clients. Keep what works and build on it. When something doesn't work, choose whether to discard that tactic or make an adjustment to your execution and test again. Over time, you will know, exactly, the specific marketing tactics that work best for you. You'll also come to learn how often you need to do them in order to hit your goals. Also, by getting into the habit of testing new ideas on a regular basis, your practice continues to grow and dominate the competition.

I wish I could tell you which marketing tactics will work best for you, but—other than giving you a menu of low-cost, high-impact tactics to try for yourself—it's just not possible. Having worked with thousands of coaches over the past decade, I can say for sure that every coach develops their own marketing systems, based on what works best for their style, talents, and preferences. Your testing laboratory tells you what works best for you.

In my own case, here are just a few things I have learned about my own results in attracting clients:

- About 75 percent of the prospects I get from referral sources become clients. Meanwhile, among prospects who hear about me through online marketing activities, the conversion rate is much lower. Perhaps 25 percent of these prospects become clients. For this reason, I have become much better at quickly qualifying prospects who learn about me online, so that I don't waste my time with people who are just looking for free coaching.

- Clients who come via referrals typically sign up for a six-month or full-year engagement. Clients who come via the Internet are much less willing to sign up for an engagement that long. Usually they want to start with a three-month trial.

- The ten best referral sources in my network send me about 80 percent of the total number of referrals that I get. Of course, I am careful to nurture those relationships, while also working hard to build relationships with more referral sources.

- When I give a three-hour seminar to 25 people, whether for a fee or for free, at the end of the seminar three to six people will want to talk to me about a coaching engagement, and two to four of them will become clients. For this reason, seminars have become one of my top business development tactics to get coaching clients.

- When I used to give a one-hour speech at an association meeting where 30 people heard me talk, I got anywhere from zero to one client—even while my speech got rave reviews. This was despite the fact that giving speeches is a great way for other coaches to attract clients. I have tried changing up my speeches to get better results, but have not had success. For this reason, when I'm invited to speak, I instead offer to do a free 3-hour seminar. That way, I know that I'm more likely to get clients.

- When I give a one-hour webinar to 25 people who are on my newsletter list, one or two of them will become clients. However, my list only grows fast enough to support one webinar every month. I need to find ways to grow my list more quickly if I want to offer more webinars.

- Ten percent of my newsletter subscribers eventually buy something from me, whether it is an information product or coaching engagement. Many of these people have also attended webinars, read my blog or book, or seen me speak. In other words, my business development activities reinforce each other.

You get the idea. There is no limit to the types of things you can test, in addition to the marketing tactics that attract the most clients:

- Different versions of your elevator speech.

- Questions to ask prospects that get them most interested in your services.

- Conversations that get a prospect to finally decide to hire you or not.

- The types of articles that get the most attention from your target market.

- Blog entries that get the most hits.

- Social media platforms that work best to attract new referral sources and clients.

- The offers on your website that get you the most subscribers and, ultimately, clients.

- Association memberships that are worth the dues that they charge, and those that aren't.

- The best way to get in the door with clients. For instance, test whether you have the most success starting with a low-cost assessment, a three-month contract, or a yearlong contract that includes a free assessment.

- The highest price you can charge so that you win 85 percent of the engagements you can pursue. You don't want to win 100 percent of the engagements you pursue, or you are charging too low. The most successful coaches win 75 to 85 percent of the engagements they go after.

Once you have enough experience and data, you can predict your revenues with a fair amount of certainty because you know how many and which types of business development activities you need to do to attract enough clients to hit your goals. Ultimately you want to get to the point where you have your business development down to a system.

For instance, the table below projects revenues that I can expect from three of my business development activities: my top referrals sources, three-hour seminars, and online webinars. For each activity, I can project a range of expected results based on my past experience. I know I can hit the low end of the projections just by doing each activity on schedule, while executing them consistently. Meanwhile, I can test new ideas to more consistently hit the upper range of these projections.

Illustrative Revenue Projections from Business Development Activities

	Top Ten Referral Sources	3-Hour Seminars	Online Webinars
Estimated # of Prospects Each Time	N/A	3–6	2–4
Frequency of Tactic	Ongoing	5 times per year	12 times per year
Total Estimated Prospects from This Tactic Per Year	15–20	15–30	24–48
Conversion Rate	75%	66%	25%
Estimated # of Clients	13–17	10–20	6–12
Revenue Per Client Per Year	$30,000	$25,000	$15,000
Total Revenue from This Tactic	$330,000 – $450,000	$250,000 – $500,000	$90,000 – $180,000

Start recording your results. Test different ways to do even better, and record what worked and didn't. Take baby steps until you get your confidence. Don't bet everything on a particular marketing tactic until you have done some small tests. Keep building on what works, and discarding or tweaking what doesn't.

There is one crucial mindset needed to have a successful testing laboratory and enjoy the benefits of a systematic business development program: You have to be willing to fail. We have all heard that Thomas Edison developed 1,000 light bulb prototypes before he discovered one that actually worked. Hopefully your experience in attracting coaching clients won't be as punishing, but you do have to expect and embrace failure.

Many newer coaches give up too soon because they can't take the stream of failures required for their coaching business to get going. Be prepared to hear the word "no" a lot. Get used to testing different ways to attract clients, and then not getting the results you wanted. I can't tell you how many rejections I have heard from prospects I wanted to work with, and how many marketing tactics I have tried that did nothing for me. When these things happen to you, pick yourself up, get as much advice as you can about how you can do better next time, and make an adjustment. Keep testing. Be willing to fail. It might take a long time to get that first client, and then that first referral, and then a full practice.

As long as you know you have a valuable solution for clients, and as long as you have the passion to be a coach, you will eventually test and fail your way to success.

Chapter Eight

THE MOST POWERFUL TACTIC IN YOUR ARSENAL – CONVERSATIONS TO GET REFERRALS

E ven the novice coach knows how important referrals are to building a thriving practice. Someone who learns about you from one of their colleagues is more likely to hire you than a prospect who comes from other sources. If they don't want to hire you, they are more likely to give you introductions to people who might. Someone they trust, or at least perceive to be credible, recommended you. Through the psychology of social proof, some of that trust and credibility rub off on you. Almost nothing makes my day more than getting a referral from a client or colleague.

Unfortunately, most coaches don't get as many referrals as they could. The main reason for this is that many coaches are too passive when it comes to asking for referrals. As a result, they sit back and hope that their clients and colleagues will send prospects and new contacts their way. Despite what some politicians tell you, hope is not a strategy. Instead, every coach needs to take a systematic, proactive approach to asking for referrals. At the same time, you need to be expanding your power base so that more and more decision makers in your field know you and are primed to send clients your way.

This chapter shows you how to get more referrals, starting with colleagues who already know you and then shifting to clients.

REFERRALS FROM COLLEAGUES.

Here is a ten-step process to get referrals from the people in your network:

One: Make time to explicitly discuss referrals.

Asking for referrals should not be something you do in passing. To maximize results, set apart some focused quality time. Take your colleague to coffee, breakfast, or lunch. Make sure that you both have your contact lists with you so you can exchange contact information if an opportunity comes up.

Two: Come prepared to help them first.

What's the best way to get a referral? Give one first. Before you meet with your colleague, anticipate how you can help them. If they are also building a professional practice, be ready to share names of people in your network who might benefit from their services. If they aren't looking for referrals, think about how you can help them in other ways. Are they looking for a new job? Would they benefit from information about trends in their industry? What introductions can you make to help them strengthen their power base? Whatever you do, don't come to this meeting empty-handed.

Three: Take the pressure off by talking about introductions as well as referrals.

It can feel as if you are being pushy by asking for referrals to potential clients. It is much easier to ask for introductions instead. At the same time, some people in your network might not feel comfortable sending potential clients your way, but almost everyone is willing to make introductions. When you meet with a colleague, gauge the relationship. If there is enough trust and rapport, start the conversation by asking about referrals, and then shift to asking for introductions if you hit a wall. If the relationship is superficial, focus on getting introductions.

Four: Educate them about the types of people you want to meet.

Don't make your colleague read your mind. Be very specific about the types of people you want to meet, and how you can help them. For instance:

- "I'm looking for technology leaders in emerging growth companies."
- "I want to meet female executives who are frustrated in their jobs and are thinking of starting up a business."
- "I want referrals to professionals who serve elite athletes, like agents, financial planners, coaches, physical therapists, sports medicine doctors, and strength and conditioning trainers."
- "I want to meet people in the healthcare industry who know lots of other people."

Five: Help them to get specific.

People sometimes need help coming up with names. You can help them help you by asking very specific questions that refresh their memories. The more specific you can get, the greater your chances of getting some referrals. For instance:

- "Who have you met recently at your church who…"
- "What about the XYZ Club where you are a member?"
- "Who lives in your neighborhood that might be…?"
- "Who is the most dynamic executive you know?"
- "Tell me about your fellow board members on ABC Non-Profit…"
- "Doesn't your spouse know someone who…"
- "Who are the parents at your kids' school that might…"
- "What are the divisions in your company, and which ones are struggling with…"

The best situation is one where your relationship with the colleague is so strong that you can ask them to go through everyone they know on their contact list, one by one.

Six: For each referral or introduction, learn as much as you can about the person.

Ask questions to understand the other person's goals, issues, communication style, and interests. Also, ask how well your colleague knows the other person. That way, you know how likely it is that the referral or introduction will be predisposed to want to meet you. Moreover, if you get lots of names from your colleague, you can prioritize and start with the people closest to him.

Seven: Figure out the best way to follow up, and take timely action.

Every time you get a name, ask for the best way to follow up. Your colleague can make the introduction, or they can give you permission to initiate contact using their name. Regardless, when you make contact, give a very soft sell. If it is a referral, email or say something like, "Hi John. Mary Jones gave me your name, and suggested I call you. I don't know whether it makes sense for us to meet or not, but Mary thought that perhaps you would find interest in the work that I do for people in your field. Would you have a few minutes to chat and see if it might make sense to have a longer meeting?"

If it is an introduction, the script becomes much simpler: "Hi John. Mary Jones gave me your name, and suggested I call you. She thought that we should meet, because we are both interested in XYZ and might be able to help each other out. If you agree, would you have time this week?"

Eight: Keep your colleague apprised.

Your colleague has gone out on a limb for you with someone in their power base. Follow up to let him know what's going on, whether something comes of it or not.

Nine: Give thanks.

Whether you get a new client, a new contact, or a big rejection, thank your colleague. Send a handwritten note. Send a tasteful gift.

Ten: Repeat.

Don't make a referral meeting with a colleague a one-time affair. Repeat the process every few months. If your colleague sent clients, or introductions, your way, do what you did the first time. If you didn't quite get the results you wanted, but you know this person knows people who can hire you or help you, learn from the last meeting. Find ways to improve the relationship. When you do meet again, change the way you educate him about the types of referrals and introductions you seek.

REFERRALS FROM CLIENTS.

With clients, referral conversations are similar to the above process, but with a few important differences.

First, there is a right time and a wrong time to ask clients for referrals and introductions. If the coaching is not going particularly well, or the client seems to be struggling through some tough issues, you probably don't want to bring up the subject of referrals. Similarly, if the client seems to be wrestling with whether or not to renew the contract, figure out how to keep the client you have before asking them for introductions to clients you don't.

The right time to ask a client for referrals is when things are going well, or when they are predisposed to really like you. Examples include:

- *When they first become clients.* While some clients might tell you to wait until they see results, many will give you referrals at the very beginning of an engagement. There's a honeymoon period when the client is very excited to be working with you, and wants to justify in his mind that he made a smart decision. You might say, "I'm excited to get going. At the same time, I get most of my clients through referrals, and I hope you don't mind my asking whether you might know others who might be interested in the same results we are working towards." At a minimum, by asking now, you open the door to have future referral conversations.

- *When they tell you that they are getting value.* That's a great time to say, "I really appreciate that. Now that you mention it, would you mind very much talking about others in your organization or network who might get similar value by working with me? As you know, I get most of my clients through referrals, so I'd really be grateful if we could carve out some time to talk more about this."

- *When you give them a referral to a new client or customer.* As soon as they thank you, you can ask them if they know anyone who might want to work with you.

- *When you make an introduction, especially at a networking meeting.* This opens up the opportunity to ask them about whom they know at the meeting.

- *At the end of every session, when you ask, "What was the most valuable part of today's session?"* As soon as they answer, you can ask them if, sometime soon, they would be willing to discuss others who might also find value. Of course, you can't do this every session you meet with a client, but every month or so might be appropriate.

- *When you take time to review progress over the past month or months, and they acknowledge the results they have been getting.*

- *When they achieve an amazing result.* After you both celebrate and acknowledge the result, and before the client's glow wears off, the time is ripe to ask who else they know who might benefit from a result like the one that just happened.

Also, it's a great idea to include a clause in your client contracts that require the client to have at least one referral conversation with you. For instance, "The client acknowledges that the coach relies on referrals to build his practice. Therefore, during this engagement, at a time when the client is satisfied with the results the coaching process is getting, the client agrees to have one 30-minute conversations with the coach about potential referrals." You only have to ask for one, because the first one opens the door to more.

Second, another difference when going after referrals and introductions from clients is in how you educate them about the types of people you want to meet. The best opening question in a referral conversation with a client—after you've discussed ways you can help them—is, "Could you tell me about the top three most valuable things you are getting from our work together?" From there, you can probe about other people they know who will also benefit from that kind of work.

However, your client might not have a complete picture of the services and value you offer, beyond the scope of your current engagement. Be sure to take time to tell them about your full range of services. Who knows? Whether they think of a referral or introduction for you or not, they might hire you for some additional work.

Third, the conversation you have with the referrals you get from clients is a bit different, because you can reference your work together. For instance, "Sue, as you know, Elizabeth suggested that we meet. She told me that she's talked to you about the results we have been getting, especially in helping her selling skills. She thought that you might find value in a similar process to the one we are following now. I have no idea if that's true or not, but would you be open to meeting or at least talking for a few minutes to find out?"

Finally, if you sense that your client is getting uncomfortable, or that you are pushing too hard and hurting the relationship, back off. Don't alienate a good client! Either shift immediately to asking for introductions, go back to asking about introductions you can make for them, gracefully end the meeting, or discuss something less controversial. You can always ask for another conversation later on when timing is better.

DESIGN YOUR IDEAL, ONE- OR TWO-CALL-AWAY POWER BASE.

By this point in the chapter, many coaches have realized that they can do more to get referrals and introductions from the colleagues and clients in their existing network. You might also realize that your network of contacts is not as high-powered as it needs to be for you to be the dominant coach in your market. If this is the case, don't fret. Instead of complaining about the network you have, design the network you want. Challenge yourself to identify, and create, the network that the go-to coach and trusted advisor in your market would have.

The top professionals in any market are one or, at most, two calls away from the opinion leaders and movers and shakers there. Take a moment to list everyone you should know and, more importantly, who should know you. Don't censor any names. Here are examples of people you might want to be one or two calls away from: the top CEOs and executives in your industry, the head of the relevant association, top philanthropists, a billionaire and a few multi-millionaires, top entrepreneurs, venture capitalists, the chairman of your local chamber of commerce, the governor of your state, the mayor of your town, the local or regional news anchor, the publisher of the local newspaper and trade journals, a radio talk show personality, the top consultants who serve your market, partners at the legal and accounting firms that serve your market, the CEOs of the other leading companies that serve and supply your target market, people who are on the boards of the most prominent non-profits in your area, the head of the economic development committee, and—just for the fun of it—a few well-known athletes, actors, and rock stars.

Don't think small when you do this exercise. Why shouldn't you be rubbing shoulders with the best and brightest in your field? Get out your database of contacts, and start writing down the names of the people who should be on the contact list of the go-to coach and professional in the field.

It is easy to dismiss the above list by saying to yourself, "What do I have that they would ever find valuable?" There is always some way you can help. I never dreamed that I would be able to partner with someone as well respected and successful as Jay Conrad Levinson, and yet you are reading my third collaboration with him. It turns out that I did have something to offer him: the time and drive to do the heavy lifting of writing the books that could expand the *Guerrilla Marketing* reach.

Similarly, I have met some top investment bankers who refer business my way. One of these bankers finds value in what I do because he likes my thought process. He appreciates the tough questions I ask about opportunities he is pursuing, and—when he needs me to—the way I hold him and the executives in his portfolio accountable.

Don't sell yourself short. There is always a way you can help. Busy and highly visible people need others who can save them time, bounce ideas around in a safe environment, and provide information that will help them.

The best way to meet high flyers is by getting an introduction to someone else who knows them. If you can't reach the person you want directly, find someone who can, and build a relationship with them. LinkedIn provides a great tool to do this. You can search for someone on LinkedIn, and then track exactly how many degrees removed you are from them. From there, you can map out the shortest path to reach them. It might take time to get to someone who will make the introduction for you, but it's worth the wait.

At the same time, many successful people are surprisingly open to meeting with up-and-coming professionals. I have met many future mentors by first asking them out for coffee to ask for advice. Pick at least one person you want to meet and ask them if they wouldn't mind meeting you so you can ask for advice—whether about trends and issues in the market, career advice, or advice about something they know about and might be flattered to share with you. Some will decline, but many will agree to meet.

Another approach is to pitch an idea to the person you want to meet. The person might reject the idea, but that rejection could start the relationship. For instance, I met one heavy hitter by telling him about an investment opportunity in his industry that I had read about. He wanted to know more. I did some due diligence, and found out that the idea was a scam. He was impressed that I actually did due diligence. "Most people don't do due diligence anymore," he told me. On that day, I earned his trust, and he has become a client and someone who sends business my way.

A third approach is to hang out where top decision makers do. In his book *Art of the Deal*, Donald Trump shares that he joined a leading social club in New York City to be able to rub elbows with the VIPs in town. Every community has a few places where the most successful people hang out. In one town north of San Francisco, there is a monthly breakfast club that is packed with the people who run that town. In your town, it might be a particular church, Rotary club, golf club, or university club. If your target market is industry focused, there might be one or more associations or conferences where you need to be.

Fourth, I've met some top executives by doing occasional research studies. Anyone can design a research study, and then interview the top people in the field for their opinions. You don't need to have a Ph.D. For instance, I worked with a colleague to interview the top marketing executives of some of the biggest technology companies in Silicon Valley. We met with executives at Oracle, Cisco Systems, and Yahoo! Once one executive agreed to participate, we used his or her name to persuade others that they needed to be part of this survey, too. By the end, we had a phenomenal set of interviews that added to our understanding of best practices in the market and—more importantly—we had developed the start of a relationship with some of the most important people in the industry.

Similarly, a colleague and I collaborated on a book where we profiled 24 super-successful African Americans. Each chapter focused on one individual. We interviewed a general in the US Army, an entrepreneur who became a multi-millionaire by age 25, a restaurant magnate, a top executive at Nickelodeon, a leading physicist, and the founder of a very successful record label. While we knew a couple of these people, in most cases we had to cold-call and invite them to be in the book. Most of the people we called agreed, and it has been wonderful to stay in touch with many of them since we completed the book.

Finally, there is no reason why you can't just call someone and tell them that you think you can help each other. For instance, a few years ago I got a call from a coach and consultant. He said, "I read about your work coaching healthcare professionals, and I think we should meet. I live nearby and do a lot of work with physicians and healthcare organizations, too." We met for lunch, and ended up collaborating on a book that helps physicians to better market, and run, their practices. Since that first meeting, we continue to help each other with leads and introductions.

VIPs come across lots of people who want to be hangers-on, so they tend to be distrustful. Build the relationship slowly. Don't ask for anything from them unless they offer to help. Stay in touch by sending articles of interest, congratulating them on their achievements, and occasionally asking for their advice about an idea. Over time, the relationship will grow.

SUGGESTED HOMEWORK:

1. Take a few moments to assess your current power base and how well you leverage it to get referrals and introductions.

2. Who is the one person you can contact right now to set up time to talk about referrals and introductions?

3. Identify at least one person who isn't in your power base, but that you should know. Develop a strategy to meet them.

4. Set a goal for how many referral conversations you will have every week, and get moving.

Chapter Nine

ALLIANCES TO BRING YOU A STREAM OF BUSINESS

Alliances are formal relationships with other people and organizations that can bring you a stream of business. Even one alliance can bring you an amazing number of clients and opportunities.

This chapter identifies the four broad types of alliances you should consider, and how to form them. The four types are: becoming a partner with companies that provide complementary services that you can offer directly to your clients; sub-contracting with companies and coaches that have more work than they can handle; developing arrangements with complementary professionals who promote your services; and forming relationships with associations and other gatekeepers to your ideal clients. The chapter ends with an illustrative list of the types of alliances that one common kind of coach, the business coach, might want to form.

ONE:

Create alliances with companies that provide complementary services, which you can offer to your clients directly. The first type of alliance is with companies that provide products and services that you can offer directly to your clients. For instance, many coaches have an alliance with an assessment tool or suite of tools, like Profiles or Myers-Briggs. Similarly, many business coaches offer their clients a service to do background checks on employees; get business financing; keep their books; generate financial reports; and find temporary or permanent staff. These alliances are important, because they beef up your capabilities, usually without adding anything to your overhead, and can generate more revenue for you. Also, if you align yourself with a strong brand, your reputation improves by association.

TWO:

Form alliances as a sub-contractor, serving as a sub-contractor to firms or individuals that have more work than they can handle. This strategy provides a good way to get your income stream going. Many large firms involved in recruiting, consulting, and coaching hire coaches on a contract basis. Do some research in your area and find out who the big firms are, and what credentials they need from you in order to consider you for future work. Look for coaches who have successful practices; they sometimes contract work out when they are too busy.

There are some downsides to being a sub-contractor. Most importantly, you don't control the client relationship, or even the scope of the work. Sometimes a client might benefit most from months of coaching, but you are only allowed to offer a few sessions. You might need to follow the coaching firm's methodology, instead of your own preferred process. You might be assigned a client who isn't very open to coaching and have to decide whether to terminate the relationship and potentially alienate the company that brought you in, or go through the motions in order to get more work later.

The best way to look at sub-contracting is as something to do when you first start out, and de-emphasize as you build up your practice. Don't let sub-contracting take up all of your time, so that you don't have time to get your own clients. Otherwise, you have something more like a job than a true coaching practice.

The bottom line: While being a sub-contractor can supplement your income, it is best to be someone who contracts out work to other coaches. That way, you control the client relationship, you control the deal, and you make the bulk of the profits while others do the work.

Case Study: Sub-contracting and Becoming a Valuable Asset to Larger Firms

Thanks to Barbara Hulick of Hulick Consulting, LLC for sharing her experience and advice about sub-contracting as a coach, consultant, and trainer.

Hulick Consulting, LLC is a woman-owned company in the Washington DC metropolitan area. The company offers a series of results-oriented programs in five key areas: Performance Management, Talent Management, Personal Effectiveness

Management, Career Management, and Executive Coaching. We also provide solutions in Human Capital Planning, Workforce Planning, Competency Development, and a wide range of human resources practices and processes.

In a crowded market, Hulick Consulting has found success in sub-contracting with larger companies. Here are some lessons learned about sub-contracting.

Determine Your Niche.

A key to sub-contracting is to figure out the skill sets and talent that the larger firms may have difficulty in developing or retaining or that may be outside their typical areas of competency. Hulick Consulting discovered that it is too expensive for many larger companies to maintain senior human resource and training competency with government experience. We have personnel with highly technical skills and years of government experience. You have to decide what you do best.

Build on Your Reputation.

All of Hulick Consulting's personnel have served as senior government managers and executives. They also have solid backgrounds and reputations for excellence. Our people have continued to develop and expand their knowledge and skill sets as the market changes. The company is not static and doesn't rest on past accomplishments. We build on our reputation by being able to tailor specific services to the client's needs and requirements, rather than depending on canned programs or approaches. You have to continue to move forward by building capacity and new expertise.

Surround Yourself with Stars.

In any professional service, you are selling your expertise, contacts, and knowledge of the sector in which you work. You have to surround yourself with superstars. You are marketing specialized talent that adds value to larger companies. You make yourself indispensable by supplying the skill sets that other companies do not have or do not want to maintain. Find good people, and form strong partnerships. We have found that the superstars know other exceptional people who can be called upon when needed. These very good people have a wealth of contacts, which can be used to expand the business into unexpected places.

Network, Network, Network.

You need to network within your industry. Join professional associations. Get to know other sub-contractors on very large contracts. They may become your partner in other ventures or may introduce you to other businesses that broaden your list of contacts. We had early success because of referrals; landing a plum sub-contract with a large corporation for a multi-year project. This project led to other work and a long list of valuable partners.

Seize these types of opportunities to provide quality work and demonstrate expertise. People will remember your work and you will get referrals.

Have Strong Ethics.

At times, you will be partnering with other sub-contractors and large contractors. At times, you may be competing with these same groups. You must maintain strict confidentiality about the proprietary information you have gained from the people and companies you have worked with in the past. You cannot divulge what you know to other companies. Hulick Consulting has won the respect of very large corporations by maintaining confidentiality, and being seen as an ethical partner that can be trusted.

THREE:

Form alliances with complementary professionals. Many other professionals serve your target market and don't compete directly with you. They also want to attract clients to their practice, and you can help each other out.

Tactics include:

Start a mastermind group.

Mastermind groups have been around at least since Napoleon Hill discussed the idea of mastermind alliances in his classic book, *Think and Grow Rich.* Many coaches swear by these groups, and yet many others still have not formed or joined one. Pick a few colleagues and meet weekly or monthly to discuss issues, make introductions, and give support.

Start a lead exchange and professional's business club.

If you have found, as I have, that many of the national lead exchange groups don't exactly put you in touch with the movers and shakers in your target market, then start your own. Create a lead exchange club in your community specifically for high-level professionals seeking to help each other build their practices. Start a business club specifically designed to help non-competing professionals grow their business; as compared to a mastermind group, which has just a handful of participants, a business club might have dozens of members.

Co-promote an educational webinar, seminar, panel, or summit.

Let's say you coach stay-at-home moms who run businesses. Why not team up with an accountant, estate planner, and business attorney, all of whom also have solutions for this market? You can market an online webinar, create a live seminar or panel, or even launch a weekend summit filled with activities and leading speakers.

Send out letters endorsing each other's services, with a special offer.

If someone came up to you and said, "I'd like to send out a letter to my entire client and prospect database endorsing your services and offering them some sort of special deal to try out your services," wouldn't you leap at the opportunity? Think of a few professionals in your network who reach your target market, and make that offer to them. In exchange, ask them if—at your expense—they would reciprocate the favor to the people on their list, with an endorsement of your services and a special offer for them. You can offer a free eBook, webinar series, or assessment—anything that you know people will find valuable and that will generate response for you.

Merge your separate newsletters into one.

One coach reports that he has merged his newsletter with the newsletters of three other complementary professionals. That way, he reaches four times as many people as he would on his own. Also, recipients get much broader and deeper content about addressing their issues.

Start an association for your target market.

Many existing associations fail to serve their members. There are also opportunities for new associations to start up and fill the needs of a particular group—perhaps a group that you want to reach. You can collaborate with a few of your colleagues to create a new association that provides valuable support, information, and research for members. You can charge a small fee, but what's more important is that you and your colleagues become gatekeepers to a large group in your marketplace. If you want to test out whether there is demand for a new association, create a group on LinkedIn with an association name, and see how many members you and your colleagues can attract.

FOUR:

Create alliances with associations and other gatekeepers to your ideal clients. Existing companies and associations can provide you with phenomenal access to potential clients. At a minimum, get active in at least one association or group that reaches your target market. Offer to speak and lead webinars. Get on the more visible and active committees, and do great work for them. Write articles in their newsletter. In this situation, you are one of many people trying to get more visible, but you should still take advantage of the opportunities that the association offers.

At the same time, seek out more formal alliances. For instance, Mike Pacholek, of Summit Assessment Solutions LLC, has built an alliance with a leading human resources group. He shares, "We recently formed a strategic alliance with a large Midwest human resources organization by introducing them to the concept of creating a Culture of Coaching within their members' organizations. The organization, plus their members, currently utilize the Profiles assessment system and our Executive Coaching services. Our ability to train and certify individuals within an organization as an Executive or Leadership coach was instrumental to forming the alliance; we developed this capability due to our relationship with The Center for Executive Coaching and its Master Certified Coach Trainer model, which gives us a license to train others to be coaches."

Similarly, Wayne Morris of Eventus Coaching has an alliance with an accounting association in the United Kingdom. Through this alliance, he has a captive audience of accountants through whom he offers free webinars, a subscription-based online program about building an accounting practice, and business coaching to accounting firms seeking to grow their businesses. In my own case, I've formed an alliance with a Human Resources consulting firm in the Philippines. They bring me in to train people to be executive coaches.

Franchises also offer an opportunity to form alliances. Many franchises have gaps in the training and support they offer to their franchisees. If you have a methodology that specifically addresses the franchise's needs, you could become a preferred vendor of coaching services. A franchise might even hire you to develop proprietary coaching content for their franchisees, after paying you a development fee.

Please note that it is not a slam-dunk to call an association, or franchise, and become the exclusive or preferred vendor. Many of the better-known associations require you to pay significant sponsorship fees to become what they call a partner. However, in some cases, you can structure a deal where you pay nothing up front but do pay some portion of the revenues you generate through the alliance.

Depending on your coaching niche, there are other alliance partners. For instance, I have had success going to local banks and offering to run free monthly meetings for their commercial clients. The banks are happy to provide space and invite their members, because they want to stand out as having unique ways to help their clients succeed. I'm happy to facilitate a monthly meeting that runs like any of the for-fee groups, like Vistage or Renaissance Executive Forums, because I get to build trust and demonstrate my credibility to the leading businesspeople in my area. Participants are usually happy to meet with me one-on-one outside these meetings to discuss their needs in more depth, and many either become clients or make introductions for me.

Similarly, every business coach should have at least one business broker as an alliance partner. Business brokers make commissions on the businesses they sell. Yet, 85 percent of businesses listed by brokers never sell. Business coaches can help by working with business owners to get their businesses in shape for sale. They can also coach the new owner during the transition phase. Meanwhile, the business broker makes more money, because he gets more businesses that are saleable, and also improves his reputation by offering after-sale services.

Take a few minutes and list as many potential alliance partners as you can come up with for your specific type of coaching and target market. Following is a list of 34 potential alliance partners that might apply to a business coach, but it will hopefully help you to come up with ideas for your particular niche:

1. Business brokers, as already noted above;

2. Accountants and bookkeepers;

3. Small business attorneys;

4. Financial planners with business owners as clients;

5. IT repair firms and installers;

6. Software developers and salespeople;

7. Web designers;

8. Search Engine Optimization providers;

9. Social media consultants;

10. Commercial bankers;

11. Venture capitalists;

12. Private equity investors;

13. Hedge fund managers;

14. Investment bankers;

15. Angel investor clubs;

16. Chambers of commerce;

17. Industry associations;

18. Rotary and other service clubs;

19. Small Office/Home Office associations;

20. Meetup.com groups;

21. Your local or regional economic development council;

22. Office supply companies;

23. Other vendors to small businesses in your niche;

24. Commercial real estate brokers and managers;

25. Temporary staffing firms;

26. Recruiting firms;

27. Professional employer organizations;

28. Benefits providers;

29. Human resources consultants;

30. Marketing consultants;

31. Small Business Investment Corporations;

32. Business insurance providers;

33. Business incubators; and

34. Colleges and universities with entrepreneurship courses or institutes.

Chapter Ten

ACHIEVE EXPERT STATUS THROUGH INFORMATION AND BY EDUCATING YOUR MARKET

The first part of the book suggests that you will do better as a coach when you think of yourself as more than a coach. You are an expert, and coaching is one of many possible ways that you share this expertise.

As an expert, you have a wonderful opportunity to attract prospects. You do this by providing valuable information to the people in your market—information that educates them about the key problems they face, and how to solve them. This establishes your credibility, demonstrates that you provide value, and builds your reputation. It compels people to get in touch with you to learn more, and at least give you their contact information. This allows you to follow up with more information and education over time. As you continue to show value, and build credibility with the people on your list, some of them will contact you to learn more about your services and products.

As you do more and more of this kind of marketing, you become known as a credible expert. People start to talk about you, even if they have never met you. Your value as a solution provider increases, attracting clients becomes simpler, and charging higher fees becomes easier.

Following are some of the best ways to achieve expert status:

PUBLIC SPEAKING.

When you speak in public, people feel like they know you, even if they have never met you. You build instant rapport, trust, and credibility.

Associations, summits, trade shows, and conferences frequently seek out speakers for their events. You can reply to requests for speakers, or send a query letter to the relevant decision maker. If you send a query letter, suggest up to five speeches and include a catchy title for each one. Then write a few sentences about what that topic covers and how the audience will benefit. Close with a paragraph about why you are the perfect person to deliver these topics. Note that you will only provide content, not make any sales pitches.

Today, there are many companies that will gladly take your money to show you how to get paid speaking gigs. Please note: the paid speaking market is extremely competitive, and—while celebrities and best-selling authors can get paid five figures for a speech—most people struggle to get by from speaking alone. To make it in that market, you need a recognized name and compelling content. I suggest that you first focus on establishing your reputation through free speaking. Once your reputation and confidence start to grow, seek out paid speaking opportunities.

There are two primary goals when you speak. First, get the contact information of everyone in the audience. The best way to achieve this goal is, at the end of your speech, to pass out a feedback form for people to fill out. The form should give people the opportunity to write down what they liked best about your speech, advice to get better next time, and an offer. The offer can be for a free eBook, special report, a free webinar, a subscription to your newsletter, or a free course delivered by email. Make your offer as compelling as possible, or else you'll lose the opportunity to keep in touch with people. Once you get the forms back, follow up with an email or even a phone call to everyone who responded. Thank them for attending and ask if they have any follow-up questions or feedback. Of course, get them whatever you promised to them as quickly as possible.

Your second goal when you speak is to get prospects. There are two keys to doing this. The first key is to have compelling content that makes the audience hungry for more. Start with a powerful opening, introduce a difficult problem that your audience wants to solve, make a few compelling points about how to solve the problem, and illustrate the points with examples and stories that keep the audience riveted. Make sure that your presentation style is relaxed, confident, and engaging. Involve the audience wherever possible. If you are serious about speaking as a way to establish credibility, watch and learn from as many top-tier keynote speakers as you can. For extra practice and networking opportunities, get yourself into a program like Toastmasters or the National Speaker's Association.

The second key is to connect with the audience so that they want to come up to you after the speech and ask for more of your time. Before you speak, survey some of the participants to ask some questions that you can reference and build into your speech; if you speak at an association meeting, you can usually get a few names and phone numbers to contact. Doing that kind of pre-work instantly sets you apart as someone who goes the extra mile. On the day of the speech, show up early to meet and greet people coming to your speech. That way, they are predisposed to feel like they know you, and it earns you their support. During the speech, take time to ask for questions and involve the audience. For instance, ask for a show of hands of people who have experienced a particular issue. After the speech, let people know that you will be available for questions, and stay as long as needed to talk to participants; thank them for coming, and set up a time to follow up with prospects who are interested in hiring you.

LIVE SEMINARS.

Live seminars offer many of the same benefits as public speaking. However, with a live seminar, you can achieve greater intimacy with your audience through exercises, more questions and answers, and the opportunity to help them solve their specific problems.

As noted earlier in this book, live seminars are one of my most successful marketing tactics. I pack my seminars with so much content that participants can't help but leave feeling like they need a coach to help them sort through the issues. In the case of the strategic planning seminar I lead, many participants realize that they need to involve their whole team to develop their strategy, and invite me in to help.

Once you get a large enough list, you can turn seminars into a product that earns you a lucrative revenue stream. Until that point, you can team up with associations and other organizations that are interested in providing valuable content to members.

Initially, seminars don't have to be fancy. You can even lead a series of brown-bag lunchtime seminars via an association, chamber of commerce, large company, local college, or commercial bank.

WEBINARS AND TELESEMINARS.

Webinars are seminars that you offer online, using widely available software to connect people from all over the world. Popular platforms include www.gotowebinar.com, Microsoft's online suite of office solutions, and Adobe

Connect. Even if you are not comfortable with the latest technology, these platforms make it easy to schedule a webinar. You can even use them to run a webinar from your office or home computer; record your webinar; and follow up with participants after the event. GoToWebinar even sends a report after the webinar telling you who was connected, for how long, and for what percentage of the time they had your webinar up on their screen instead of doing other things on their computers.

Teleseminars are talks that you give by telephone, using a bridge line. Many companies take advantage of some arcane telecommunications laws to be able to offer you free bridge lines, and even free recording and downloading. Examples include allfreeconference.com and freeconference.com. The latter company lets you do a free non-recorded teleseminar, and charges you to record it.

There is no magic in planning and marketing a webinar or teleseminar. First, come up with a catchy topic that your target market will find of value. As with speeches and seminars, you can start by persuading an association or other organization to sponsor your event. For instance, for my career coaching practice, I have led a number of webinars about career success for students and alumni of major universities. The career centers of these institutions always look for experts to provide helpful career advice to their constituents.

Alternatively, if your list is large enough, you can promote the event on your own. Let the people on your list know about it; spread the word via your social media contacts; tell relevant associations about the event and ask them to publicize it to their membership; and ask colleagues to spread the word to their list. For a webinar, design a PowerPoint or other presentation to show on screen. If you don't know PowerPoint, go to www.elance.com and hire someone to help you. Once you have content developed, you are ready to lead the event. Try to keep the event to less than 30 minutes. Attention spans are shorter for virtual meetings. After the event, follow up with participants to get their thoughts and ask whether they would like to speak more about their issues.

Because you can record webinars and teleseminars, you get an instant product that you can post on your website or even sell.

PODCASTS AND VIDEOS.

Record audio lectures, or podcasts, about topics of interest to your target market and post them on your website. All you need is a microphone and simple sound recording and editing software, like the WavePad Sound Editor, which is available through NCH. Save your recordings in mp3 file format, which is currently the standard file format for downloading to mobile devices.

You can also record videos and post those on your website and on YouTube. Technology is so inexpensive today that you can create high-quality videos without hiring an expensive production company. Just get a friend or colleague to record you. You can keep recording until you do the perfect take, or invest in some simple video recording software. Once you have enough video content, you can create your own channel on YouTube, and let your target market know about it.

ONLINE RADIO.

Many coaches have started up online radio shows, especially through the site blogtalkradio.com. This site lets you set up your own radio show, schedule shows, host shows, take calls, and download shows for use elsewhere. The site is free for basic services.

Set a regular time to do your show, and find guests who want exposure. The site radioguestlist.com lets you look for guests, and you can also search the Internet for relevant experts and reach out to them. That way, you become an expert who interviews experts.

As your show grows, so does the traffic to your radio show's page, and this, in turn, will bring more traffic to your regular website. You can download a recording of your show and upload it on your website, giving visitors even more reason to view you as a credible expert.

If you don't want to host a show, at least make yourself available to be a guest on shows. Reach out to online shows and tell the host why you should be a guest. Be sure to get a recording of the show so you can post it on your website or at least link back to the show so that visitors know you are a sought-out expert.

ARTICLES.

Writing is an important way to establish credibility. There are so many forms of media available today, both traditional and online. As soon as you put down this book, get online and do some research about all of the publications and websites that reach your target market. Then follow the same process you would if you were trying to get a speaking gig. Write a query letter that describes five article ideas with catchy titles, along with why you are the perfect person to write them. Send them to the editor of the publication you are targeting, and follow up. If you get a positive response, write the article. If you don't, ask for advice about what kinds of articles they would like and how you can be more successful next time.

Once you get one article in a publication or on a website, nurture the relationship so that you can submit more. At some point, ask if you can become a regular columnist or blogger.

There are also thousands of free article submission sites that let you post articles. Examples include www.evancarmichael.com, www.ezinearticles. com, and www.buzzle.com. You can also register as a contributor on Yahoo! Do a search on Google to get a list of the most current and popular article submission sites.

Note: If you can't find a journal or website that publishes articles specifically to your niche, start one. What better way to establish yourself as an expert and, perhaps, generate a new stream of revenue?

Make sure that any articles you write have a quick sentence or two about you and a link to your website. This is most commonly placed at the bottom of your article. For instance: "Andrew Neitlich is the Founder and Director of The Center for Executive Coaching, a leading executive coach training firm. For more information, visit www.centerforexecutivecoaching.com." On free article submission sites, people can link back to your profile, which has a link to your website.

One key to getting your articles accepted is having a strong title, and therefore, a compelling topic. Take a look at the leading journals and websites in your industry, and study the article titles that are most featured. Examples typically include:

A top five or top ten list: "Top ten technology trends in the real estate industry"

A step-by-step article about how to solve a problem: "Five steps to resolving conflicts in a family business"

Common mistakes and how to avoid them: "Five mistakes you are making that are causing you to get fat"

Dirty secrets: "The dirty secret about getting a raise that your boss doesn't want you to know"

Little-known ways: "Little-known ways to improve your marriage"

Piggybacking on popular news topics: "Three lessons from the recent sex scandal"

Reviews of new products or books and how they relate to your target market: "Why every bowling alley owner must see *The Big Lebowski*"

Interviews with well-known experts: "An interview with Warren Buffet about the three keys to small business growth"

Of course, you can also post articles on your own websites, along with executive briefs of up to three pages, or white papers of ten to 15 pages that go deeper into a topic than the typical article.

BLOGS.

Every coach should have a blog on his website, and update it at least two or three times every week. Blogs give your website dynamic content, which search engines like to see when they are ranking your pages. Each blog entry gives you a reason to get in touch with your list and social media contacts, and invite them to come to your website and read your blog.

Blogs are easy to set up, and any website designer can get you started. Make sure you have analytics for your blog, so you can see which blogs get the most attention.

In addition to writing your own blog, work to get a gig as a blog writer for a high-traffic site that reaches your target market. Don't forget to contact complementary professionals with blogs, and offer to write a guest post. Even a single guest post adds a link to your site, and exposes more people to what you have to offer them.

PARTICIPATION IN ONLINE GROUPS AND FORUMS.

Get involved in LinkedIn and other groups/forums that focus on your target market. If a LinkedIn group doesn't exist, or isn't targeted exactly right, start one. Get active by posting discussions, and responding to posts that others make.

Be sure to be positive on LinkedIn. Don't get involved in an online fight with another group member, or you will both come out looking bad. Take the moral high ground. Acknowledge others for their contributions, and only post when you have something productive and informative to add.

YOUR NEWSLETTER.

Your newsletter becomes a key medium to invite people to read your articles, see you speak, come to your webinars, and visit your blog. It also gives you another platform to send valuable content to your list.

Constant Contact, at www.constantcontact.com, along with iContact, and GrowthPOD, among other companies, lets you set up professionally designed newsletters and send them to your list.

Another powerful option is a platform like www.1shoppingcart.com, which lets you send out broadcasts to your market whenever you have something new to share. It also has a tool which lets you set your list up on auto-responders. Auto-responders are automated messages that go out in a set sequence you determine, regardless of when someone signs up. For instance, if Joe signs up today and Mary signs up next month, both get the exact same series of messages, one day, three days, five days, twelve days, and fifteen days—or at whatever interval I choose—after they join. Auto-responders let you write something once, and send it out again and again to your list. This means that everyone has the same experience. Then, when you have something fresh and new to say, you can send that out as a broadcast to everyone on your list.

Many people wonder about how often they should send out a newsletter or auto-responder message. The answer is that it depends on how long your newsletter is. Longer newsletters should go out every two or three weeks. Short newsletters, designed to provide quick tips, can go out weekly or even every couple of days. You can run tests to figure out what works best for you and your target market.

The key to a good newsletter is valuable content. Write great material for your audience. Don't give them fluff. If you are an executive coach, nobody on your list wants your brownie recipe or stories about how hard it was to move to your new home. They also don't want a constant barrage of sales pitches. Give 99 percent great content. If you do make offers, make sure they are for low-risk, valuable ways for people to learn something they care about.

RESEARCH.

One of the most powerful ways to establish your credibility is by performing occasional research studies about, and for, your target market. There are a couple of benefits to doing research. First, if you design your project right, you get access to some of the leading people in your target market, without having to sell them anything. Second, you develop valuable intellectual capital that no one else has. This helps you stand out as a coach compared to the competition that doesn't do research. It also makes it easier for you to pitch speaking and writing gigs, because you have unique content.

You can do research through an online survey tool like Survey Monkey. This will give you terrific content that you can analyze and turn into a professional presentation. However, it is better to design a research study where you get to talk to participants face to face or by phone. That way, you develop the relationship with your participants, which is one of the benefits of research in the first place.

You can even do a research study on behalf of an association. For instance, a non-profit association engaged me to interview 50 executive directors about the main challenges they face in leading a non-profit organization. I met 50 new potential clients, and then presented my findings to the members of the association. This single research project landed me at least a dozen clients.

You don't need a degree in statistics or a Ph.D. to conduct research. Keep it simple and qualitative. For instance:

- Interview some industry leaders about their top challenges.
- Do research about the top technology trends in the industry.
- Collect case studies about the most important moments, or hurdles, in the careers of leaders in your market and how they handled them.
- Ask about the hiring needs of a sampling of businesses in the market.
- Do a study about best practices about a specific issue.
- Benchmark employee turnover in the field.

You can also perform a quantitative study, for instance, by creating a simple index. Ask participants to rate something on a scale of 1 to 10, such as their confidence about the market for their products, and then report the average, along with the distribution. Give the index a catchy name, repeat it every month or quarter, and report the findings to relevant media. There are all sorts of indices published every day in a variety of news media—about employment, hiring plans, salary increases, bonus plans, consumer confidence, and feelings about the economy. Why can't you create and promote an index, too?

QUESTION AND ANSWER SITES.

There has been an emerging online trend in question and answer sites like: eHow, Mahalo Answers, Yahoo! Answers, Amazon's Askville, Yeddle, AllExperts, Answerbag, wikiHow, and WikiAnswers. You can attract some interest by monitoring relevant questions on one of the more heavily trafficked sites and answering them. You can also have a colleague ask questions on your behalf, and then answer them. I've tried this strategy myself, and the results have been mixed, especially when compared to participating in LinkedIn Groups and other niche-specific forums. However, it is worth some investment of your time to continue to monitor these sites, and to test whether you get a bump in interest by participating as an expert.

INTERVIEWS IN THE MEDIA.

Publicity experts cost a lot of money, and don't guarantee results. You can get interviewed in newspapers and journals, on websites, on radio, and even on television, with a little elbow grease on your part. First, make sure you get media requests every day from sites like helpareporter.com, reporterconnection.com, and radioguestlist.com. While many of the requests in these publications are from small-time outfits, every once in a while a reporter from a big media outlet wants to interview an expert like you. Regardless, reply to any and all requests that fit your expertise. Make sure your response answers the request precisely, because you are competing against hundreds, or thousands, of other respondents.

Second, collect contact information about the reporters and radio show producers in your market. These people are inundated with requests, so you have to build the relationship over time. One way to do this is by sending out frequent press releases with tips or advice about a current topic. Always remember to follow up by phone. Be patient and follow up over time to build trust and establish your credibility. Make sure that you can tell your media contact in less than a minute why you have something that their audience will want to hear. A minute will literally be all the time you have to explain that you are an expert with relevant information about a topic that is in the news, or that the journalist is covering. If you strike out, try again with a new idea later.

When going for interviews, be willing to start small. It is much easier to pick up the phone and call your local television station, radio station, and beat reporter than to reach out to Good Morning America, Rush Limbaugh, or George Will right out of the gate. Be patient, and build your platform over time.

CREDENTIALS.

If you've got them, flaunt them!

Credentials won't necessarily get you hired, but they do add to your credibility and can get you in the door. Large companies and government divisions are increasingly requiring coaches to have a coaching designation from the International Coach Federation or a credential from one of their approved coach training companies. In addition, many coaches are seasoned professionals with credentials in business, psychology, spirituality, medicine, law, and counseling. You can also feature awards, degrees, memberships, and anything else that shows that you are a professional with a deep commitment to coaching and the target market you serve.

Some coaches are a bit obsessive about collecting credentials. Don't go overboard. You can't hide behind pieces of paper forever. Credentials don't make the phone ring. You still need to get out there and get visible as an expert and competent coach.

YOUR PRODUCT PORTFOLIO.

A wonderful thing happens when you start creating products and programs, like books, information packages, assessments, and seminars. Just one product or program will give you credibility as an expert. A second one adds more, and a third still more. Each new product that you launch reinforces your reputation, and helps your status as an expert continue to grow ever upwards. The great thing about this tactic is that you don't need a full client roster to get started with this tactic.

Later this book will show you how to choose and get going with your portfolio, in ways that don't require nearly as much work as you think. For now, give some thought to one or two products besides coaching that you think you would like to roll out to your market, and that you think will work well in your niche.

GET STARTED NOW!

Please don't let the above list overwhelm you. There are many, many ways to educate the people in your market and show that you are a credible expert with valuable insights. You don't have to do all of them. Pick one, and do something. Then pick another, and do something. Keep building on what works, and learning from what doesn't. Keep expanding your arsenal of tools to establish yourself as the go-to professional in your market. Take one step at a time, and keep moving forward.

Chapter Eleven

INTERNET MARKETING TACTICS

nline marketing, also known as Internet marketing, digital marketing, web marketing, or e-marketing, is still in its infancy, continues to evolve daily, and might intimidate coaches who haven't grown up with the likes of LinkedIn, Facebook, and Twitter. However, using the Internet to market and promote your coaching services is much too powerful to ignore. With the right online marketing tactics, you can reach a targeted and highly focused audience from around the world—quickly and inexpensively (often at little or no cost).

This chapter lays out a best-practice strategy for how you can use online marketing to your greatest advantage. It breaks down your online strategy into two components. First, it discusses your website, including your blog and newsletter. Second, it isolates social media and explains how to use these technologies to drive traffic to your website, generate leads independently, and build an interactive community around your "brand."

While the advantages are incredible, many people who are not familiar with the mechanics of online marketing frequently interpret it as elusive, complicated, and confusing. They are intimidated and tend to shy away from it altogether. Some people even think that there is some sort of secret silver bullet to mastering this channel. If only they knew this secret, millions of visitors would come to their website. A slew of online marketing professionals are delighted to reinforce this view, which adds to the frenzy.

Truth be told, online marketing is very straightforward and easy to initiate. There are no magic formulas to uncover, nor is it complicated to learn and understand. The real trick is focusing on the key things that have the greatest impact for you, and having the discipline to do them consistently. In other words, keep it simple and stay the course. Don't let yourself get distracted by all the options and buzzwords. There are hundreds, perhaps thousands, of online tactics available to you, but most of them won't get you results. For this reason, the advice that follows emphasizes the 20 percent of tactics you can use to get 80 percent of your online results. Why not get more while doing less?

START WITH YOUR HUB.

Optimize your website, blog, and newsletter. A good coaching website has three goals that reinforce one another. First, provide high-value, low-risk offers to visitors that require an opt-in or sign-up so that you are able to collect their contact information. That way, you can follow up with them over time and continue to demonstrate your value. Second, establish yourself as a credible expert with valuable solutions to offer the people in your target market. If you achieve these goals, the third and ultimate goal—getting clients—follows.

Given these goals, a best-practice coaching website includes the following features, most of which should be visible right on your home page:

1. *A clear message in language that resonates with your target market:* Many, many coaching websites present the coach as yet another generic, plain vanilla coach. That's because most coaches haven't laid a solid strategic foundation, as recommended in the first step in this book. Before you create your website, make sure that you have a clear and compelling message to a specific target market. That way, visitors who come to your website will immediately be interested in content that they care about.

2. *A headline or tagline with a compelling primary benefit:* Hook your prospect right away with a reason why they should check out the rest of your website. Your visitors make a decision to stay or go in less than a second. Persuade them to stay with a great headline that arouses curiosity, reminds them of their pain, or gets them salivating over an opportunity. For instance, "Chief Nursing Officers: Stop struggling to develop nurse managers…"

3. *A compelling offer to capture contact information:* While you should have lots of free, no-obligation content on your site, you should also have one or more offers for information. These offers should require the visitor to at least leave their first name and email address. It is not enough to say, "Sign up for our marketing newsletter." You have to offer more value than that. A better offer would be, "Get $10,000 worth of FREE tips about how to increase your sales by at least 10% in 30 days."

4. *At least one testimonial up front and center:* Your website needs at least one great testimonial right at the top of the website. Sprinkle testimonials throughout the site, not just on a dedicated page. Add some audio and video testimonials, too.

5. *A memorable look and feel:* Make the website memorable. For instance, one of my favorite coaching websites is Marc Pitman's www.FundraisingCoach.com. Take a look at it. His logo includes a photo of himself with a memorable red bowtie. He also dots the 'i' in *fundraising* with a red bowtie. The tagline in the logo, "Fundraising is an extreme sport," is also compelling. In fact, everything on the site establishes his brand, along with his expertise, in an unforgettable way.

6. *Valuable information and tools:* You increase your credibility if you develop a few, simple informational products that visitors can buy or download for free. Offer a short eBook, some videos, a step-by-step guide, and/or an assessment tool. Show a graphic image of one of them right at the top of your home page, so people can click it for more information and also see that you are more than a fly-by-night coach.

7. *Links to social media:* Add links to your Facebook, LinkedIn, and Twitter accounts, so that people can join your network and follow you there. This also helps to build your online reputation, which is invaluable in today's digitized world.

8. *Easy navigation:* Go back to www.FundraisingCoach.com for a moment. While Marc has the usual navigation buttons to see his bio, learn about his services, and contact him, he also has three large boxes that visitors can click. One is for people new to fundraising. One is for experienced fundraisers who want to get re-energized. The last is the title of his book, *Ask Without Fear!*, a title that is compelling in and of itself and encourages people to click.

9. *A great blog:* Update your blog regularly with fresh, interesting material. Don't hide your blog on a back page of your website. Instead, make it visible, front and center on your home page. That way, visitors are drawn in and want to read content that is most relevant to them.

   Your blog becomes an important way to let everyone in your network know that you have just released new information—whether it's an announcement of an upcoming event, special news or a general post covering a topic of interest. With every blog entry, use Twitter, LinkedIn and Facebook to notify your network and invite them to check out what you have written. Offer an RSS option (Real Simple Syndication), a web feed that allows others to quickly access your content in a standardized format. Your web designer can show you how to have all of these things working together, so that you can update your profile on one and have it instantly update the others.

10. *Social proof:* Use every form of social proof you can to build your credibility. For instance, if you have been interviewed in major news media or a book, post the logos as part of a "Featured in…" section of your website. Post videos of any television interviews you have done, along with links to online interviews. List high-profile clients, assuming you get their permission. Include testimonials from opinion leaders in your field. Highlight any awards you have won that are relevant to your coaching capabilities.

11. *Multimedia:* People process information differently. Some like to read, some like pictures, some like video, and some like audio. Offer all of these options on your website. For instance, create a series of short videos of you speaking or going through a PowerPoint presentation. Camtasia software lets you record your screen while you speak, whether with a video of you or a PowerPoint.

12. *Events:* A section of your home page should let people know about upcoming seminars, speeches, webinars, teleseminars, interviews, and book releases. Link these announcements to pages with more detailed information.

13. *Multiple services:* As you have read before, think of yourself as more than a coach. Offer multiple ways for people to get results, including training, consulting, and speaking.

14. *Easy ways to get in touch with you:* Don't just offer an automated contact form. Include multiple ways for people to contact you: office phone, cell phone, Skype, email, and instant messaging.

15. *Personal touches:* People want to hire people they like. Provide a thumbnail photo or two of yourself and your team, if you have one. Throw in a personal fact or two about yourself in your bio. Don't provide too much

personal information, which often gets people uncomfortable, but do provide enough to come across as a genuine human being.

Once your website meets the above criteria, drive traffic to it via every activity you do:

- Anywhere you speak, tell people to go to your website for a free report or more information.

- Anytime you write something, include a link back to your site.

- If you post a video on YouTube, have an online radio show, or do anything else online, add a link back to your site.

- On the back of your business card, offer a free special report available on your website.

- When you meet people, ask them if you can add them to your newsletter list. Also invite them to go to your website to get a free report.

- Use your newsletter and social media presence to drive people to your website when you post something new and valuable.

- Make sure your website address is listed in your social media profiles.

- If you offer a certification or training, create a graphic and ask graduates to post the graphic on their sites with a link back to your website.

- If you write a testimonial for a colleague or blurb for a book, include your web address.

There are also three for-fee opportunities to drive traffic to your website. The first is Search Engine Optimization or SEO. SEO consultants use a variety of techniques to have your site come up as high as possible in search results on Google and other search engines. When people search on sites like Google, they are much more likely to click on a listing that is natural, as opposed to a paid listing. SEO consultants claim to understand the algorithm that search engines use to rank websites, so that they can make your site show up higher than your competition.

There are many self-proclaimed SEO experts on the market, and unfortunately not all of them are good at what they do. Some are no better than scam artists; they take your money while making false claims about the results they are getting for you. Others practice their craft in a way that seems more like voodoo than science, and can't seem to provide the results that get you more prospects and clients.

If you choose to hire an SEO firm, talk to lots of providers before you make up your mind. Get at least three references from each, and ask those references for specific results that they achieved. Test the accuracy of their statements by searching for them on Google. Searching using the keywords they say have been optimized will very quickly reveal the accuracy of their claims. Ask specific questions to test their understanding of the search engine algorithms and how they will help your site do better. Test their approach by asking other potential providers for their assessment of their tactics; vendors are brutal when it comes to picking apart their competitors' SEO tactics. Challenge each potential vendor to tell you which key words they would focus on, and what it will take for them to get your site at the top of the search engine rankings for those words.

Search engine algorithms change all the time, and so do the strategies that SEO providers use. For a time, the hot idea was exchanging links with another site. However, search engines now cancel out these reciprocal links. Then some firms started doing triangular links, where you get a link back from a site, and your SEO firm creates a landing page that provides a link back to the other site; that way, you avoid the reciprocal link problem. Unfortunately, search engines figured out how to identify and neutralize this strategy. They penalize pages that are nothing more than link farms. A current trend is to create landing pages with unique website names that have relevant key words, and attract traffic back to your site.

Instead of fretting about all of these strategies, you can do a lot of the SEO work yourself. You can check traffic statistics about your site, or any site, by using www.alexa.com. Choose a few key words that you think your prospects will search for, and use them liberally—but not so much that it is clear you are gaming the system—in the first 250 words of your home page. Update your blog frequently, because search engines like sites with dynamic and original content. Original cannot be overemphasized. Do the things that get links back to your site; like becoming a guest blogger on high-traffic sites and getting involved in groups and forums. Write articles and submit them to free article posting sites like ezinearticles.com, and participate as an expert on question-and-answer sites such as Answers.com and Quora.com.

A second for-fee strategy is pay-per-click or PPC, where you pay only when someone clicks on your ad. Google AdWords and the Microsoft Ad Center offer this service, as do Facebook and LinkedIn. These services let you target your ads to specific key words, geographies, and demographic groups. You choose your budget, and can track results by who signs up for your newsletter or who buys a product online. You can also test different ads to see what works best for you. While these services are worth a test, you can end up paying a lot of money for a single click, especially if you rely on expensive key words. Don't make the mistake of confusing traffic to your site with conversion to clients; you can spend a fortune to get thousands of visitors and never actually get a customer.

If you use any of these services, start small and test. Set a specific daily budget, or you might be in for a nasty billing surprise. Don't mention coaching in your ads. Instead, talk about how you help to solve a big problem in your target market. Get them to click by making them interested to learn more. Offer a valuable free report or assessment tool. Tell them about the specific benefit you provide. Test lots of ads and keywords, and weed out the ones that don't get you any conversions to newsletter subscribers or buyers.

The third for-fee strategy is paying to get your website listed in a relevant directory. If you can find a directory that has a terrific page rank with Google and other search engines, it can be worth the investment. It will bring you traffic, and also improve your own page ranking, because search engines look at the quality of links back to your site. Just make sure you get proof that the directory really does get great traffic, because there are always scammers who are more than happy to take your money for a link on a site that is simply a ghost town.

Of course, the best ways to drive traffic to your site are the free ones, and using social media is one of the best.

USE SOCIAL MEDIA EFFICIENTLY.

Focus on the big three plus one niche opportunity. Creating an effective social media presence is simpler than the many social media consultants want you to believe. The keys to success are don't be intimidated, and don't get involved in so many social media sites that you feel overwhelmed. Focus on the big three—LinkedIn, Facebook, and Twitter—plus one niche opportunity depending on your target market. Then test other social media sites once you are getting results from those.

Let's start with LinkedIn. Every coach needs to have a profile on LinkedIn—a business-to-business social networking site. Before you write and/or post your bio, share it with some colleagues and get their advice and feedback. When ready, make sure to fully complete your profile, including a link to your website and other social media accounts. Invite your colleagues to be part of your network. Use the endorse feature on LinkedIn to ask people to endorse you by writing favorable testimonials. Get active in relevant LinkedIn groups where the people in your target market stay in touch, or start your own.

As you meet new people, especially ones who are decision makers in your field and add to your credibility, ask them to become part of your LinkedIn network. When you have news to announce—about a new blog post, seminar, interview in the media, or anything else that your network will find interesting—update your LinkedIn status and post in some of the more relevant LinkedIn groups. LinkedIn also has a question and answer feature that can further establish you as an expert in your field.

The free LinkedIn service works perfectly well for most coaches. However, if you want to reach out to more people in your target market than are in your direct network, you might want to test their premium service. Recruiters and other professionals who rely heavily on direct marketing are primary users of LinkedIn's premium service. It may or may not be a fit for you. Before signing up, make sure you have taken the free LinkedIn services as far as you can.

Now it's on to Facebook—the behemoth of them all. Something to keep in mind—Facebook is a more social, personal network that people largely use to stay connected with friends and family. You might not want potential clients seeing pictures of you burning the shish-kebab at the family reunion—or worse. However, many coaches use Facebook with success to market their coaching practices and books. That's because Facebook offers an option that allows businesses and professionals to create distinct "pages" to promote their products and services. These pages are completely independent of personal profiles, which is good news for those of us with opinionated Uncle Daves or photo-crazy Cousin Marshas.

Facebook pages have many features, in addition to the usual Facebook abilities to post news, send messages, and connect with people. For instance, if you have a book, you can post excerpts, positive reviews, and links where people can buy it. Therefore, if you are new to Facebook and don't have the time to learn about creating a page, hire someone who knows. There are many high school kids who live on and breathe Facebook day in and day out. They can create a great page for you on the cheap. Once you have a professional-looking page for your coaching business that ties in with the rest of your branding efforts, ask your friends to "Like" it. You need a certain number of people to like it in order for you to obtain a unique URL and be more visible. So you want to ask people proactively for their help.

Next up—Twitter. Twitter offers unique opportunities for the savvy coach. Every time you have news or something valuable you have posted online, you can let your followers on Twitter know through updates known as "tweets." Tweets need to be 140 characters or less, so you need to get creative when posting. You can also send out frequent tips and pieces of advice that position you as an expert with something worthy to say. And what's nice is that you can send these directly to other Twitter members via direct messages (DMs) or by using the "@" reply feature.

Many people think that success on Twitter means having millions of followers, like Shaq or Lady Gaga. For coaches, quality is much more important than quantity. Your goal should be to connect with the opinion leaders and decision makers in your target market. You can follow them and hopefully they will follow you in turn. Also, when people visit your website, some will click your Twitter link to follow you. As you build your network of followers, post frequently to stay relevant.

Twitter creates an overwhelming amount of noise, and you want to cut through the clutter with content-laden messages to a specific target audience. As with Facebook, if you don't know how to use Twitter, hire a high school or college student who does. This is especially important with Twitter, because there are ways to get penalized on that site, for instance, by following or unfollowing too many people at one time or sending too many DMs. Also there are many scams offering to build up your list of followers—some for a fee—and you want to avoid these. Build your network slowly and organically for best results.

Your fourth opportunity is to get active in specialized social media sites that target the people in your niche. For instance, Idea Health & Fitness Association's Fitness Connect is a social media network for the fitness and health market. Most associations also have their own social networking member area. A simple

Google search will get you a list of the relevant social media opportunities to connect with people who might be interested in your coaching practice.

These four tactics can take plenty of your time, to the point where you really don't have more bandwidth for other social media sites. In my own case, I confess that I don't even have time to do the above tactics justice. I write my own blogs and post them on my websites, but that's it. I have hired a social media freelancer to get the word out about them to my social media networks. She handles my Twitter accounts, maintains my Facebook pages, and lets me know about new LinkedIn groups. This arrangement works just fine for me, and is well worth the cost.

TIME TO TAKE ACTION.

Don't read the above and have it be academic. Answer the following questions, and upgrade your online marketing:

- How can you improve your website so that it is a best-practice coaching website?

- How can you improve your LinkedIn presence and network? For instance, how can you get more testimonials and endorsements? Which new group will you join or start?

- Do you have a Facebook page? If not, when will you create one? If so, how can you make it better and encourage more interactions?

- Are you active on Twitter? How can you improve the quality of your followers and use Twitter to drive more traffic to your website?

- Are you active on a niche social media site targeted to your market? If not, what will you do about it?

- Plant a seed today and watch the results blossom in no time at all.

Chapter Twelve

LEADERSHIP TO BUILD YOUR CREDIBILITY

y taking on leadership roles, you put yourself in contact with other leaders. As long as you do what you say you will do and get results, you show others how effective you can be. Many coaches—along with consultants, attorneys, accountants, and other professionals—get a good share of their clients by being active in their local trade associations or in their communities.

There are a few criteria in choosing a leadership role.

- First, choose something that you want to do. That way, it is easy to follow through on your commitments while also coming across to others as engaged and enthusiastic.

- Second, avoid organizations and roles that might polarize your target market. For instance, political organizations and non-profits that focus on highly charged issues might not be the best be—unless, of course, you are specifically targeting groups that support those issues.

- Third, don't simply join an organization and dabble in it. Become a leader by finding the most visible and important committee or project, and getting active on it. Show people what you can do!

- Fourth, pick a role and an organization where you will meet the kinds of people who will help your practice. People understand that volunteering is not purely altruistic. You have to find value, too. Many organizations attract people with lots of time who love to talk and don't have much going on in their lives. Avoid these.

Following is a menu of just some of the leadership opportunities available to you:

NON-PROFIT BOARDS.

Well-connected people tend to serve on non-profit boards, and are willing to make connections for other board and committee members. Take on a project, like leading a fundraising event, and you can impress people with your abilities. For instance, Elene Cafasso, President and Head Coach at Enerpace, Inc., shares, "I serve on the Board of the University of Chicago Women's Business Group, and have gotten three clients I can directly attribute to my Board Service. Two of the three are board members who got to know me well from working together. They hired me for my honesty, expertise and passion for getting things done. The third client is a male CEO of a manufacturing firm. He saw my name listed as the planner of many of my group's events and reached out for more information. I've also had many speaking opportunities by working with this group and have had the opportunity to build relationships with several other professional organizations on behalf of my group."

SOCIAL CLUBS.

Find the most active Rotary or other social club and become an active member. While explicitly networking for business is frowned upon in such organizations, members of these clubs get to know each other well, and they also want to help each other succeed.

GOLF, TENNIS, AND FITNESS CLUBS.

If you play golf, tennis, or another sport, get active in a local club. Play in leagues. Sign up for tournaments and other club events. However, make sure that the way you play sends a positive message. At my tennis club, one member is an up-and-coming professional and a fine player. Unfortunately, when he plays, he gets into some sort of competitive zone where he gets combative with his opponents. It often reaches the point where it is embarrassing for him and not many members want to play with him. I know that I'm never going to hire him after seeing how he conducts himself on the court.

ASSOCIATIONS.

Join whichever association serves your target market. The key is to get active and be a leader. Serve on committees or get on the board. Write, speak, and do research. Start a new interest group or committee if you identify a need that plays to your strengths. For instance, Mary Shafer, Principal of The Word Forge, works with small publishers and independent authors. She shares, "Over the past year, I've gotten many new clients through the visibility of my position as president of the Mid-Atlantic's regional publishers' association."

If there is no association serving your target market, start one! You become an instant gatekeeper and leader in your niche. You can also start a Meetup.com group. Meetup.com lets you create a group of like-minded people who meet locally to network and share common issues.

CHAMBER OF COMMERCE COMMITTEE OR BOARD.

Assuming the Chamber of Commerce is a good place for you to meet people in your target market, don't just join your Chamber and go to the weekly networking meetings. That's only the start. Become an ambassador, and welcome other members. Get on a visible committee. Work your way up to a seat on the board.

YOUR LOCAL ECONOMIC DEVELOPMENT COMMITTEE.

Many communities have Economic Development Committees that try to attract and retain business in the area. If you target business owners, this committee often has some of the most prominent businesspeople involved. Find a way to get on it.

TOASTMASTERS.

Toastmasters is an incredible group. Aside from helping us improve our speaking skills, it can get us in front of some terrific people. Teri Johnson, C.P.C., Business and Executive Coach, shares, "I hold a leadership position within my local Toastmasters group as Vice President of Membership and Mentorship. This visibility has led me to a few clients over the years I've participated. One, in particular, was a woman whose career choice wasn't working for her, since she had lost her enthusiasm for the work. During the course of our work together, she put together a one-year plan to get her certification in personal fitness training and launch a new business, which she did. She's now very happy with the role she plays in people's lives and might not have otherwise sought out a coach, but she heard me speak about bringing a sense of purpose to work and found resonance with that and hired me. She has since referred others to me."

VOLUNTEER TO PUT TOGETHER A MAJOR COMMUNITY EVENT.

Most communities put on a few annual events that everyone goes to. There are races, parades, holiday celebrations, county fairs, and festivals. Get involved. You will meet terrific people, they'll see what you can do, and they'll introduce you to others.

CITIZEN TASK FORCES.

In many communities, citizens can participate on task forces to provide input on issues. For instance, my town has a task force of citizens who give input to the police department about crime and community relations.

PLACES OF WORSHIP.

If you are religious, get involved in your church, synagogue, or wherever you worship. Help out at the school. Get involved in a mission. Help out with a group. Get on a board committee or on the board.

YOUR CHILD'S SCHOOL.

Most schools push hard for parents to get involved, and some require it. Since you are going to be involved anyway, why not get the most out of it? For instance, one of my colleagues is a business coach who specializes in marketing. He is very active in his child's school, and has gotten a few clients by networking with other parents who happen to run businesses.

YOUR CHILD'S AFTER-SCHOOL PROGRAMS.

You can make terrific connections by getting active in your child's sports league, arts programs, or whatever else your child does after school. Become a coach or assistant coach. Volunteer on game days. Get involved in fundraising. You will meet like-minded parents, and perhaps meet some clients, too. I have a friend in Silicon Valley who has met executives and CEOs of some of the top technology companies there, simply by getting active in his son's soccer league.

Chapter Thirteen

Chapter Thirteen

CREATIVE STRATEGIES TO REACH
TOP DECISION MAKERS AND VIPS

M any coaches wish they could reach more of the top decision makers and VIPs, and turn them into clients. These are the high-flyers who might not be in their network now but who could be highly visible clients—the kinds of client who add to their reputation in the market. Wouldn't it be great if there were some sort of magic script and step-by-step approach to attract people like this?

Unfortunately, no such silver bullet exists. The key is to be someone who decisions makers in your market want to know, and there are only three ways to get there. First, you need to get visible in places where they can learn about you. Second, you need to show that you provide something that they value. Third, you need to have a presence that tells them you are credible, authentic, professional, and committed to solving their problems.

The tactics described so far in this book are your best ticket to getting in front of them:

- Craft a marketing message that persuades them to take interest in what you have to offer.

- Get visible as a credible expert who addresses the problems they care about, so that they want to contact you, and you don't have to chase them. Speak at places they go when they are looking for new ideas. Write compelling articles in publications that they read.

- Ask them to participate in a research study that they will find relevant and valuable.

- Create a web presence that they can't resist.

- Get active in the business and social places where they hang out.

- Form alliances with other professionals who are already working with them.
- Build up your network so that you can get introductions to them.

When you do meet a top decision maker, you need to be ready. These folks do not suffer fools, and will dismiss any coach who doesn't quickly engage with them and show value. For instance, I am working my way into one very large organization, making connections in preparation for an eventual meeting with the CEO. One of my sponsors in the organization gave me some simple advice: "Andrew, if you see him clench his jaw at any point in the meeting, you know you are dead—and he's been known to clench his jaw and end a meeting two minutes in. Be patient and don't go into that meeting until the time is right and you are ready." Thanks to his advice, I am gradually meeting with my contacts in the organization, learning everything I can about the CEO's strategy and aspirations, and testing out different approaches for making the case about how I can help. Meanwhile, my sponsors are looking out for when the time is right, and slowly planting seeds with the CEO that I might have something valuable to offer him and his company.

In addition to the tactics already described in this book, following are a few ideas that might work in some cases:

THE PLANNED COINCIDENCE.

One coach's entire practice took off when he landed an executive at a major technology company as a client. He learned that this executive went for a run every morning at 6 am at the company's campus. So, every morning at 6 am, this coach started running around the campus, too. After about a week, he just happened to roll into the parking lot at the same time the executive was getting ready to start his run. The two ran together, and by the end of the run, the executive was ready to discuss an engagement.

THE UNIQUE GIFT.

It can be expensive if it backfires, but you might consider sending a unique gift to get an executive's attention. If you know they love old cars, send a handcrafted replica of a classic auto. If you know they are a Civil War history buff, send a rare Civil War history book. Include a hand-written note telling them that you are sending the gift because you are committed to working with them, and request a meeting. If you have a unique craft that you make or dessert that you bake, you can also get noticed by sending that as a gift. For instance, one professional bakes custom-made gingerbread houses and gives them to prospects as a way to stand out.

THE UNIQUE DIRECT MAIL PIECE.

There are a variety of creative mailings you can send to specific clients to stand out. For instance, design the front page of your local newspaper or, for business and executive coaching clients, the *Wall Street Journal*. Write a newspaper story dated in the future, with a headline and article about the great success the company or your target client has achieved. The story copy should describe how his relationship with your firm led to this amazing success story.

Alternatively, blow up a page from an industry directory to poster-board size, and mail it to your target client. Circle the names of the companies with whom you have worked, and a quick blurb about the results you have gotten for them. Then highlight the target company's name and write: "When do you want to enjoy similar results?"

THE TARGET-PROSPECT STRATEGY.

The biggest professional services use this strategy to go after the clients with whom they want to work. Basically, they develop a list of up the 100 people or companies they want as clients. Then they create strategies to get hired by them. You can do the same thing, although for a solo coach, 15 to 25 prospects is probably more than enough.

First, choose 15 to 25 prospects with whom you'd really like to work. Your strategy is to reach out to them at least once a month in ways that they won't find intrusive, and try to build the relationship over time. If someone on your list becomes a client, replace them with another target prospect. If another tells you they are not interested under any circumstances or, over time, becomes less appealing to you as a client, replace them with another target client.

There are many ways to reach out:

- Send them an article you have written, and ask for their feedback. Tell them that, because you know that they are an opinion leader in the industry, you would appreciate their advice.

- Ask them to participate in a research study you are conducting about best practices in the industry.

- Send them a letter that describes the value you have brought to a similar individual or company, and ask if it would be worth a five-minute call to see if the prospect would benefit from the same results.

- Invite them to a seminar or conference where you are speaking.

- Send a signed copy of your book, if you have one.

- Send them an article about the industry that they might find of interest.

- Subscribe to SoundView Executive Book Summaries or a similar service, and send them ideas from the most recent business books.

- Send a letter or email congratulating them on a recent achievement or article in the paper.

- Ask to interview them for your blog or for an article or book you are writing.

- When appropriate, follow up on any of the above activities with a phone call and ask them if they would like to meet.

Meanwhile, work behind the scenes to meet people who know them and can make introductions.

It will take some time before you see the results of this strategy, and you have to be consistent. Done well, it can be a great way to attract clients that you might not normally get to work with. Also, you control your own destiny by choosing the clients with whom you want to work.

The one caution with this strategy is that you can't overreach, or you will be perceived as no better than a spammer or, worse, a stalker. Be patient, and take it slow. Make sure you are bringing value in every interaction with them.

Chapter Fourteen

SPECIAL REPORT—GET THAT FIRST CLIENT

T he first client can be the hardest. After that, many coaches report that growing their practice becomes much easier. In this special report, coaches share how they got their first client.

Karen McMahon, CPC, ACC, Certified Divorce Coach:

I reached out to the court mediator who had brilliantly negotiated my personal child custody agreement with my ex. I told her that I was studying to be a life coach and would like to talk to her about her thoughts in regards to divorce coaching. Her feedback was enthusiastic. Unaware of other divorce coaches, she felt that so many people needed support and guidance, but not necessarily emotional therapy to help them. I asked if she would keep me in mind for any clients who crossed her path whom she thought I might be able to help. Within two weeks I had landed my first divorce client. That client is still with me, and I now have a full schedule with 70 percent of my clientele entering in the midst of or post-divorce and working to move forward in their lives.

Lillian Lambert, Author, The Road to Someplace Better: From the Segregated South to Harvard Business School and Beyond:

I got one of my early clients as a result of a speech I made at an "Economic Empower Summit" for a business group in Kansas City last fall. I was there for the day and was assigned a lady to be my hostess to escort me to places I needed to go. She is a radiologist and had left her position at the Veterans Administration Hospital and started a medical imaging company that was somewhat stagnant. We hit it off well and she asked if I would mentor her, which opened the door to offer my coaching services. It was not long before I knew that her aspiration for the business had waned. She recently sent me a recommendation stating, "Lillian's coaching skills inspired, encouraged, and set me back on task to achieving my goals."

Donna R. Hyatt, Hyatt Coaching:

I met my first prospective client at a marketing seminar where a well-known expert outlined the individual customized marketing strategies for each attendee. We connected over the course of the day and several weeks later, when she was ready for further business guidance, she contacted me. She was ready to sign on, and there was no selling on my part, as we had already established that I could help with her needs. All of my clients have come through the face-to-face networking process, either directly or through referrals. The connection is made, and the rest follows.

Lorinda Clausen, Owner, Clausen Consulting, LLC:

A trusted colleague of mine recommended me to a company that was looking for someone to administer a Myers-Briggs assessment to the Vice President. I'm a certified MBTI Practitioner. I met with the VP for a Myers-Briggs consultation and suggested he sign on for a three-month coaching gig. He agreed—mostly because he was required to do so for an Individual Development Plan that the owner had outlined for him. After the second month of coaching, he began to present situations that were slowing down the growth of the company. Being a solution provider, I suggested strategic planning and offered to facilitate. They agreed to a 2-year strategic planning commitment to the tune of $30,000. Using Andrew Neitlich's Elegant Strategy framework, we developed an amazing map for expansion of the company while also building the individual and team leadership skills of the VP, President, and Owner. The VP also loved the coaching so much, he signed on for a year. As time went on, more problems in the company arose, and with that, more of my solutions! Eventually I created a Leadership Development Plan for their top eight leaders, which included a number of assessment tools. From these assessments came the need for some skills development, and with that, a coach. I am now doing executive coaching with all eight of the key leaders in this company, and as a bonus, I provide monthly leadership seminars, which we hold over the lunch hour. I recently signed a one-year coaching contract with them and expect more of the same throughout the next several years. The three best parts? I absolutely enjoy being their 'trusted advisor.' I get paid to do what I love! I have the best boss on earth (me).

Ian Santos, Coach, Philippines:

I have established a strong backbone with my former colleagues in the companies I worked for. In fact, many of the colleagues whom I have personally mentored have become successful senior leaders in multinational companies. So, I am offering my services first to these people, and my very first client is a subordinate who has become a National Sales Manager in a big corporation. I love to talk about how I first got paid, and that is through a free lunch! I do not charge my former colleagues cash as I want to spread the word through them by giving them complimentary coaching sessions.

Cynthia Samuels, CAS, CEO and Head Coach, Inspired Multifamily Services, LLC:

Following the marketing plan of networking with everyone in my market niche and volunteering to speak and to educate people, I joined the Welcoming Committee that educates new members of the Atlanta Apartment Association. I reached out to each new member to invite them to subscribe to my newsletter, which is written specifically for the property management vendor/suppliers in the beautiful Peach State. Through that communication—which included my website address, LinkedIn address and my LinkedIn Group address—I pulled people to view my profile and/or website, and then I invite them to join my closed group. My first client is a small businessman who is a new member of the Atlanta Apartment Association with the goal of plugging in and growing his business within the property management industry.

Chad Rudolph, Business Coach, www.ChadRudolphCoaching.com:

Ross, a CPA, became my first client. Three or four things happened that made this work: First, I got the referral from a Financial Planner friend, which brought implied credibility. Second, I ran a workshop that he attended, and I actually drove him and another prospect to the event in my car, so we had very good dialog time during the drive. And finally, my car is an Audi A8L with black interior and exterior. It is a very high-end executive car. They were both impressed… the car was saying, "This is a successful guy."

Graham Side, Founder & Principal, GuidePoint Advisors:

My first client came to me as a referral from my accounting firm at the time. When I first started as a business coach, I had no visibility and little reach within the community. So it made sense to leverage relationships I already had in place that could help on both counts. My first stop was my accountant, a partner in a medium-sized, well-respected local accounting firm. He was familiar with my background and knew me personally. He was kind enough to set up a meeting with all the partners and gave me the opportunity to make a presentation to them about business coaching, the practice I had joined, and my services. Soon after that meeting he referred me to a client of his, the owner and president of an engineering and manufacturing firm that designed and built automated assembly equipment. After two exploratory meetings with the prospect, and a complimentary coaching session, he signed on for a yearlong coaching program. We worked together almost weekly for well over two years up to and through the sale of his business to a competitor.

Michael E. Frisina, Founder of The Frisina Group and Author, Influential Leadership: Change Your Behavior, Change Your Organization, Change Health Care:

I began creating relationships with health care organizations through their human resources and education departments. I began to offer a series of behavior-based teaching programs for continuing education credit for health care professionals. After having made a connection as a competent educator on behavior-based topics, I offered myself as a coach to the organization for individuals who exhibited specific behaviors that were disruptive to unit cohesion, teamwork, and collaboration. My first engagement was with a senior nurse executive, then with a vice president of quality, and then with a physician leader serving as a chief medical officer.

D. Yvonne Rivers, Chief Success Coach, The Phoebe Group:

I approached the local economic development office of my city and proposed that a workshop be created for new business licenses holders, and all others who may have attended economic development sessions. We created a flyer, as a joint venture between my company and the city. We also did an email blast to our lists. I also did several press releases and got some coverage in the local newspaper. About 25 businesses attended and I received my first two clients, a dentist and a medical transportation company. I also got referrals from my *Art of Networking* CD that I sold at the workshop.

Rich Moore, President, Rich Moore, Inc.:

I am an executive coach for CEOs, with a specialty in marketing. My first gig came via tragedy. I was working long hours as an executive, when my wife died suddenly and unexpectedly. I had three kids and needed control over my schedule to support them. I started my own business, thinking it may never work, but tried by necessity. I began by trying to voluntarily help others in a small way. For example, I offered to venture capitalists that I would be happy to visit a company and talk with them/their CEO if they ever needed a free assessment of their situation. They would take me up on the offer and set up a visit where I would talk with the CEO and executive team and give them my opinion of what needed to be done. Pretty soon, whenever the question was asked, "Who in the area is good at providing objective advice on strategic issues?" my name would come up. Board members would refer CEOs to me. My first engagement came when a CEO tried to hire me. I said no, but would provide advice part-time. So we did.

Almost all of my coaching gigs came via the same manner. Each engagement has grown out of backing off from an offer where they want to hire me and I say, "No, but I can help you part time as a trusted advisor and coach." And so, each client begins with a feeling that they are lucky to get me, a setup for success.

Didi Zahariades, MA, Psychotherapist/Executive Coach:

I knew I could never work professionally out of my home, so with a minimum budget I opened my first office. While I was in the process of renting the space, I was asking questions of the building manager when I discovered there was a need in their management team. I continued to ask questions about their staff until I was able to gather enough information to pitch my services. It started out with coaching one manager and led to coaching the entire team! As always, a coaching relationship is built on being a good listener first. Ironically, I ended up doing most of my coaching over the phone, although without the space I don't think I would have been centered enough to stay on task.

Marian Thier, Expanding Thought®, Inc. and author, COACHING CLUES: Real Stories, Powerful Solutions, Practical Tools:

I was facilitating a Leadership program at one of the three big auto makers. The head of Learning and Development approached me and said, "You seem to be good with teams, and I have this very dysfunctional cross-functional team of executives that you might be able to help. Don't worry; you can't make them any worse." I spent about six months working with them, mostly on how to be collaborative decision makers. They improved dramatically and that was my first coaching assignment. That was before there was even a profession called Coaching. Once I figured out my model for coaching, I wrote a book to share my learning. The book has been an excellent entree into getting new clients.

Craig Hohnberger, ActionCOACH Business Coaching:

My very first client was my dentist, who I landed while getting a routine checkup and cleaning. I had just left the corporate world and was just a few weeks out of my initial training to start my business coaching practice. When I gave the office manager my new insurance card, she asked what I was now doing, so I explained and asked if the dentist had ever used a similar service. She shared that the dentist had used a few practice management groups in the past but still needed help. So I asked more questions about goals, and she then asked me if I use current employees' ideas, which I do. I explained and asked what her biggest ideas were. She shared lots of great information about her ideas and the dentist's goals and challenges while I drilled down further and emphasized those were all areas we focus on. She got excited and said the dentist definitely needed to work with me, so I asked if she could do a simple favor and mention to him to ask about my new gig. He inquired while I was in the exam chair and, armed with all the information from his office manager, I jumped right into asking about his goals and needs. That Friday, we met, signed agreements, and I collected my very first check in my new coaching business. It was a perfect case study for me, as a new coach, on the power of being in the present and asking the right questions and gave me a huge jolt of confidence that I was in the right place.

Crystal Williamson, CPC, www.coachingwithcrystal.com, transformational business coach and technology/computer coach:

I volunteered to do laser career coaching at a job expo. One person I spoke to was a female attorney, over 40 years old, who was transitioning. I spent the allotted 15 minutes with her and then moved on. I thought nothing unique or unusual about her becoming a client. The next day she called, we made an appointment, and started coaching the next month! We coached for six months and are still in touch four years later!

Janis Cline, Performance Coach, Thinking Blocks Coaching Services:

I was working with a woman from my Toastmasters group who invited me to her business networking group. She thought it would be a great way for me to grow my business. The networking group met once a week and had anywhere between 7 and 25 business owners participating at a time. After my fourth meeting, a woman approached me and asked me if I could help her with some issues she was having with her employee. We sat and talked for almost two hours. She told me that she was very impressed with me and found me to be attentive and kind. She hired me and I worked with her for eight sessions over three months, invoicing her monthly. Pleased with her results, this client plugged me into her networks and many of my next paying clients came from her referrals. For me, I've found the best form of advertising is a happy client!

Tina Feigal, M.S., Ed.; Owner, Parent Coach, Trainer/Center for the Challenging Child, LLC:

I was a school psychologist working in a suburban school setting in MN. I was frustrated because as I evaluated children for emotional behavioral disturbance, I realized that a lot of it could be resolved if I could just get to the parents of these kids with techniques that work instead of the typical "yell and punish" that people were using, which only made the situation worse. I found a guy online in Arizona who had written a book I resonated with, so I contacted him and said, "How would you like me to start the Minnesota version of your business?" He said, "Yes." With an unknown name and an unknown approach, we attracted 140 people for a daylong seminar in July. I knew there was a need, so I offered myself as a local resource after he returned to Tucson. My first client called me, and we got started on making her child's behavior a LOT better. Eleven years later, I am using "Let's make 'parent coach' a household name" as my mantra. I have had such incredible success teaching parents techniques and perspectives that are extremely effective.

Step III
CLOSE ENGAGEMENTS

If you follow the guidance so far, you will attract prospects. Now, you have to turn them into clients. Some coaches do all the right things when it comes to their strategic foundation and their approach to get visible, but they just can't seem to close a deal and get paid to coach people at the price they want. Closing engagements requires the ability to engage prospects authentically, have open and honest conversations with prospects to figure out whether there is a good fit or not, develop a solution that works for both parties, handle any objections with finesse and grace, and explicitly ask for a decision. Once you know how to close engagements, business development becomes easier, more natural, and even fun.

Chapter Fifteen

OVERCOME LOW-PRICING SELF-ESTEEM

It is hard to close deals if asking for enough money is a problem for you. Simply put, do you suffer from low-pricing self-esteem? It is a common malady among coaches, and can sometimes prove fatal. The main symptom is that you charge less than you are worth.

There is an enormous range of pricing for coaching services, even for the same type of client and coaching solution. For instance, I know some business coaches who charge as little as $200 a month to meet weekly with a client, and some who charge $7,500 for the same scope. The difference is that one coach has low-pricing self-esteem, and the other doesn't.

Following are fourteen principles for curing this condition:

One: Recognize the costs of low-pricing self-esteem.

Low-pricing self-esteem is an expensive condition. You make less than you deserve, and that hurts. You feel frustrated when other, less competent coaches make more money than you. Perhaps worst of all, if you charge too little, discount your services on request, or offer free coaching; your clients don't respect you, or see you as being on equal footing with them. Ouch!

Two: Know your value.

If you want to charge what you are worth, you have to know your value. What are the costs of the problems you solve for clients? What are the benefits when they go from where they are to where they want to be? What are the clear-cut business benefits you provide? What are the emotional benefits that clients get from your coaching? You have to know. In business and sales coaching, it is relatively easy to hone in on improvements in sales, profits, productivity, employee retention, and the value of the business. Even if you offer a softer set of benefits, you need to figure out what those are and what those are worth to your clients.

Three: Ask questions so that the client understands your value.

Help the client understand the value you provide by asking probing questions, until the value you provide makes your fees look like a bargain. Books like David Sandler's *You Can't Teach a Kid to Ride a Bike at a Seminar* and Neil Rackham's *S.P.I.N. Selling* show you how to do this. Every coach needs to have a set of questions that drill down into the costs of the client's problem and the value of a solution. For instance, suppose a prospect comes to you because he can't get his team to do what he needs them to do. Examples of questions that can help you get to the true value of a coaching solution include:

- What are examples of projects that haven't been done on time or on budget, and what are the costs to the company of those?

- What is the turnover rate among your management team? What does it cost to hire a new manager?

- How do customers perceive this issue? What is this costing you in terms of customer loyalty?

- How is this problem helping the competition? What are you losing in terms of your market share and reputation?

- What is this doing to your relationship with your boss? What are the implications for your career?

- If you could get your team to do what you need them to do, what would that mean for the sales of your company? The profits? The stock price?

- What is this costing you in terms of your personal life? How is your sleep? How much time are you spending with family?

Four: Hold your ground and be willing to walk.

You don't have to win every single engagement. In fact, if you turn 100 percent of prospects into clients, you are charging too little. By holding your ground, clients have more respect for you. I have found that, when I am willing to walk away, I end up closing more engagements than when I cave in to the prospect's requests, and offer discounts. Prospects are attracted to coaches who command respect. You don't have to be arrogant about your pricing, but you can certainly be strong.

Five: Get out of the hourly rate trap.

If you charge by the hour, you instantly become a commodity. Charge based on the solution you provide. To do this, you first have to work with the client to get clear on goals and the end results. Then charge a rate that gives the client a return worth five to ten times the value of that result. For instance, offer a six-month or one-year coaching program that addresses the client's key issue and helps them achieve their goal. Quote a fee for the whole program. Of course, the client can pay in monthly or quarterly installments, but the key is that they are paying for a solution, not hours.

Six: Develop focused, deep solutions for a target market.

Coaches who are generalists have a harder time charging high rates than specialists. By offering unique solutions specifically for your target market, you make yourself more valuable.

Seven: Avoid competitive bidding situations and get more sole source engagements.

If you spend lots of time working through Human Resource departments, or responding to Requests for Proposals, you are likely to be seen as a generic-commodity coach and won't have as much flexibility with your fees. Instead, focus your business development activities on getting referrals from your network, and on establishing yourself as a go-to expert in your field. That way, you get many more sole source opportunities and can charge higher fees.

Eight: Offer other programs and products so that access to you becomes more valuable.

Imagine that you have a range of programs in addition to one-on-one coaching, including: books, information programs, group coaching, and contract coaches trained in your methodology. Essentially, people pay more money to get more direct access to you. They can pay a few dollars for a book, where they don't get to meet you at all. They can pay a few hundred dollars for an information program, where they can hear you on a monthly telecall with hundreds of other people. They can pay thousands of dollars and get access to you through a group coaching program, or to work with one of your certified contractors. Finally, they can pay top dollar to get one-on-one time with you. If a prospect balks at your prices, you can refer him to less expensive options that you offer. By having a portfolio of products and programs, access to you becomes more valuable.

Nine: Only take jobs where you are sure the client can get a five to ten times return on your fees.

I tell clients up front that we should work together only if we can come up with a justification worth a strong return on investment. If we can't and the value isn't there, why waste each other's time any further?

Ten: Raise your rates over time.

Over time, a coach becomes more confident in his worth. He sees results with clients, has case studies proving his value, and feels more comfortable charging more. He can also test higher prices gradually, until he hits a wall. That happened to me. I have increased my rates ten times since I first started out, without really changing much about the way I coach. I've simply come to realize the value I provide, and have raised prices a bit with each new client. The market will tell you when you have gone too high, and you shouldn't hold yourself back based on your own limiting beliefs and assumptions about what people will pay.

Eleven: Stop pushing your passion over client value.

Some coaches are more like evangelists than coaches. They are pushing things like leadership, authenticity, and transformation—things that they care a lot about but aren't necessarily things that other people seek or are willing to pay lots of money to get. Focus first on what your clients perceive to be of value, like having more time, making more money, feeling more confident, having better marriages, having more obedient kids, and advancing their career. Sell those things first, because that's what your clients want, and are willing to pay for.

Twelve: Be willing to get a no.

Some coaches are so afraid of rejection that they give away their services. You have to be willing to get a no. In fact, to be successful in this business, you have to be able to get lots of no's. A no is a good thing. It means that you don't have to waste any more time with a prospect who is never going to hire you, or with prospects who hem and haw and never make a decision. You can move on to a client who sees value in what you do and is willing to pay your fees.

Thirteen: Negotiate on terms, not rates.

While you hold your ground on price, be flexible on other issues. Time the payments to match their budget cycle. Scope out a coaching engagement that fits the amount of money your client can authorize without going up the hierarchy. Reduce scope to match the budget they do have. Throw in some value-added services, like an assessment tool.

Fourteen: Test a ridiculous price every once in a while.

I have a friend who started as a high-school drama teacher and now makes about $1.5 million as a coach, consultant, and trainer in the leadership communication space. He and his team work with Fortune 500 companies from around the world and command $30,000 for two days of his time. I asked him how he got up the confidence to ask for that much money. He replied, "My first client said she wanted to hire me for a weekend retreat, and asked how much I charged. I had no idea what to ask for, because I had never done anything like this before. I had no business experience and no frame of reference. So I looked my client in the eye and asked for $30,000. She accepted, and I've been charging that ever since." In other words, his complete naiveté about pricing made all the difference. Meanwhile, much smarter coaches make a lot less. Be naïve. Test a ridiculous price every so often and see what happens.

Chapter Sixteen

ASK QUESTIONS THAT ENGAGE AND ASSESS FIT

I f you do everything covered in the first two parts of this book, prospects should come to you and be interested in learning more. Some will never become clients, because they don't have the budget, don't see value in your services, or are just looking for free advice. Others will hire you. At this point in the process, your job is to engage prospects and figure out whether or not they are likely to become clients. You also have to ask yourself whether you want them as clients. That way, you can spend your time efficiently, and not feel like you are chasing after prospects who will never become clients.

There are three questions you have to answer to determine whether or not it is worth investing lots of time with a prospect:

1. Is there a real opportunity?

2. Do they want to work with you?

3. Do you want to work with them?

Before answering these questions, there is one other thing that you have to do during this phase, and no book can teach it to you. Successful coaches have a talent for engaging with other people, being present, listening for who they are and how they perceive the world, and connecting authentically so that they feel comfortable opening up. In International Coach Federation lingo, they have the ability to develop trust and intimacy, even before someone becomes a client.

There are some surface behaviors that show you are doing this. Subtly mirror the prospect's body posture and gestures. Adapt to the pace and rhythm of their speech. Make eye contact, and focus your full attention on them. Paraphrase what they have said to confirm that you understand. Show empathy, and reflect back their feelings about the situation.

However, it goes deeper than that and extends to how you create a personal bond and relate to other human beings. For instance, Sharon Hart, CPCC, and Owner of In Alignment Coaching, gives a great example of how to do this when she shares how she got her first client, and every client since:

"I landed my first coaching client the way I have connected with nearly every coaching client, through a personal connection with an individual. I was attending an event at my daughter's school and overheard a mom I didn't know explaining to her friend how overwhelmed and out of control her schedule was. The woman led a busy life as a mom, wife, and as the leader of a foundation. Her sense of anxiety and urgency continued to build during the conversation. Eventually, I had the opportunity to strike up a conversation with this woman and listen to her. She told me how overwhelmed she was, but didn't know where to find the right help. I gently encouraged her to release any feelings of guilt, and to instead celebrate her courage for being open. I also let her know that I was a coach and that, if she felt comfortable, we could connect again soon for a complimentary initial session. This seeming 'meant-to-be' encounter eventually led to our working together for two years. I have found that being open, authentic and willing to connect with another person is the best way to attract clients and build relationships with others."

Do you have the ability to establish this level of trust and intimacy with someone, even on a first meeting? If you do, you are already well ahead of the pack.

QUESTION ONE: IS THERE A REAL OPPORTUNITY?

Assuming you do have the ability to connect with others, you still have to ask the right questions to fully engage a prospect and convert him or her to a client. The first question is whether or not there is an opportunity. To answer this question, there are four things to consider:

- Is there a compelling problem that is costing the prospect enough to justify your fees?
- Do they have the money to pay your fees?
- Do they have the authority to hire and pay you?
- Is the timing right?

First, is there a compelling problem that is costing the prospect enough to justify your fees? Every coach needs to get skilled at asking open-ended questions to uncover, and put a spotlight on, the costs of the prospect's problem. If the problem isn't costing the prospect enough for them to feel an urgent need to address it, then you aren't going to get hired. That's because the prospect won't perceive enough value in your services.

Depending on the situation, costs can be related to one's business, organization, team, career, personal aspirations, and emotional state. In the previous chapter, you saw a business-related example of a set of questions to ask to uncover the costs of a problem.

As a second example, suppose that you are a parent coach, and someone comes to you because their child is out of control. Here are some questions you might ask to figure out if they are serious or not:

Question	What You Are Listening For
How long has this been a problem for you?	If this has been a problem for a long time, they might not really be serious about making a change.
What are your reasons for making a change now?	Do they have a compelling need to take action now, or are they just looking around for an easy answer out of guilt?
What are the effects of the child's behavior on your marriage? What about on the relationships with the other siblings and you, and among themselves?	Listen for this area of pain, drill down to really understand what the prospect is facing, and show empathy.
What are his teachers saying? How much time do you have to spend time managing issues at school?	Ditto.
How is this affecting your sleep, eating, mood, level of anxiety, and general wellness?	Ditto. Note that each of these categories could be covered in single questions.

Question	What You Are Listening For
How is the child's behavior having an impact on how your family spends time together during general free time at night, on weekends, and on vacations?	Ditto.
What impact is the problem having on you and/or your spouse at work?	It is important to explore all aspects of the prospect's life.
How does this problem make you feel when it comes up? How much time do you spend worrying about your child's behavior?	These questions get at the emotional costs of the problem.
What does your spouse say about the problem? How does he/she feel? What about other members of the family—grandparents, siblings, etc.?	Listen for conflicts, finger pointing, and guilt. All of these drive a need to change the situation. Note that this question is similar to a previous question about the marriage and family relationships, but takes a slightly different angle. It might uncover other issues.
What else have you tried? What has worked and what hasn't?	If they have tried things before, you know they are serious about solving the problem. However, you also want to confirm that they aren't dabblers going from one silver bullet to the next.
If you don't do anything about it, what will things look like in a year for you, your spouse, your child, and other family members?	This question magnifies the issue by extending it out in time. You can then ask about a five-year and ten-year time frame.
What are other consequences of the child's behavior?	Listen for costs that you hadn't considered.
What is your biggest fear about the problem?	Fear is a very uncomfortable emotion. This coach might also ask about whether the prospect feels anger, guilt, shame, and sadness.
What do you think are the biggest obstacles and challenges to a solution?	The more obstacles there are, or the more daunting they are, the more likely the problem is significant.

Question	What You Are Listening For
If you could wave a magic wand and make anything happen, what changes would you make?	Questions like this allow the prospect to see possibility, even in the face of enormous obstacles. The coach can also determine how big the gap is between the situation now and the desired future state. That tells the coach whether there is enough of a gap to make a coaching engagement worthwhile.
What would it be worth to you if this problem went away?	This question challenges the prospect to put a value on a solution to the problem. If the prospect has no idea, you have to ask more questions to help. If their answer is much less than your fees, it could be that more probing questions from you will help them see that the problem is costing them more than they thought. Or, if the value isn't there, let them know that there may not be a fit and, if they agree, move on.

The above questions, and whatever specific questions you need to ask prospects in your unique coaching niche, are not always comfortable to ask. They are designed to uncover costs and emotional pain so that you know your prospect has a problem big enough to justify your fees. However, you don't have to feel like a sadist when you ask these types of questions. The goal is not to make the prospect feel horrible, or like there is no way out. While you ask these questions, you have the opportunity to empathize, listen, and reassure. Later on in the process, you can design a solution that gives the prospect confidence in a better future.

Regardless, you have to be sure that the prospect has a problem that is big enough, costly enough, and emotionally painful enough to justify your fees. Otherwise, you are wasting your time. The value is either there, or it isn't. If you get the sense that the prospect is dabbling, looking for free advice, or shopping around, you have every right to be open and honest about it. For instance, when I get that sense, I am very comfortable saying, "Can I be honest with you?

Having worked with lots of people on these issues, I'm pretty good at knowing when someone is serious about making change and when they aren't. I don't get the sense that your problem is serious enough for you to want to do what's required to change." Then I shut up and wait. The other person will either agree, or offer me new information that will change my mind.

Even if someone has a serious issue and will find value in an engagement with you, that still doesn't mean there is a real opportunity. There are still three more questions to ask.

The next question is whether the prospect has the money to pay for your fees. This can be an even more uncomfortable question to ask about than the previous one, because many coaches are uncomfortable talking about money and fees. But you have to do it. It is frustrating to spend time with a prospect who seems totally engrossed in how you can help and then, at the very end, they say, "Wow! Coaching sounds great. I just can't afford it right now." It is best to bite the bullet and have this conversation early.

There are a couple of ways to raise the issue. You can ask what their budget is, but often they have no idea. One simple way to talk about budgeting is to say, "Well, it seems like you have a pretty serious issue and want to solve it. I can help, but I'm not sure if my fees are within your budget…." Then present a range of fees that you charge, and ask directly, "I don't know if those fees are what you are willing and able to pay. What are your thoughts?"

The money is either there or it isn't. If it isn't, you can suggest creative ideas to stretch out payments, reduce scope, or start when funds arrive—but after a certain point, the only option is to move on and not waste any more time.

The third question to answer to assess whether there is a real opportunity, after uncovering pain and discussing budget, is whether your prospect has the authority to hire you. No matter who you coach, they almost always have to check with someone else before hiring you. If you do any form of life coaching, the prospect will have to check with a spouse or a significant other, if they have one. If you coach executives and managers, they have to check with their boss, board of directors, business partners, or purchasing department. Early on, ask a simple question: "Who else is involved in deciding whether to move forward?" Then you can ask a bit about the decision-making process and what it will take to get their approval. As with money, if you avoid this question at the start, you might get stung after investing lots of time.

Finally, an opportunity is only real if the prospect wants to start now or at least within a very short time frame. After you have asked about their pain, budget, and decision-making, the next question to ask is, "When would you want to start?" If they don't tell you that they want to start immediately, or very soon, then something is wrong. You have already determined that they have a big problem that is costing them enough to justify your fees. They have the money. They have the authority to hire you. If they don't want to start now, it is very possible that they have not been truthful about some of their other answers.

When this happens to me, I am open and honest about my concerns, and say, "That's not the answer I expected. I thought you were committed to making a change and addressing this problem, which you said was very costly. What did I miss?"

It might be that they have a legitimate reason for a delay, such as an even more compelling priority. If that is the case, then you can ask whether you can help with the current priority. You can also probe about which priority is really more important and try to influence them to reverse their priorities or consider handling both issues simultaneously.

More often, if the client is not ready to start now, they probably are: skeptical, have some additional considerations, don't want to work with you and are too polite to tell you, don't really have the money, or aren't as serious about solving their problem as they have claimed. They may or may not be honest with you about their reasons for delay, but now is the perfect time to probe about each of these areas anyway. Ask them straight up about each issue, even if you feel like you are covering old ground.

In this situation, you can also share, "In my experience, when someone delays now, after we have taken all of this time to talk and agreed about how serious this problem is, you are probably never going to move forward. Are you sure there isn't some way we can start sooner rather than later and get this problem out of your life for good?" From there, if they still don't want to start, you can go into coach mode and remind the prospect that nothing happens without a commitment to action. Do this while reassuring them that you would love to work with them, and that you are confident you can help them get results quickly and effectively. If they still want to delay, there isn't much more you can do but agree to follow up when they say the timing will be right.

QUESTION TWO: DO THEY WANT TO WORK WITH YOU?

By now, you have the answer to the first question, which assesses fit: Is there a real opportunity? If there isn't, you can move on. If there is, you can move on to the second big question: Do they want to work with you?

Two things must be in place for a positive answer. The first was already covered at the start of this chapter. The prospect has to have enough of a connection with you in order to enter into a coaching relationship with you. Without that connection, your prospect will not feel comfortable opening up to you and sharing their most pressing issues. Coaching is a highly personal, intimate process. It is not like buying a car. Before a prospect commits, they have to trust you and like you enough to want to work with you.

Second, you need to show, and they need to agree, that you have a solution that will get them the results they seek. You have spent time with the client uncovering their pain, and now you need to show them that there is a light at the end of the tunnel. Now is the time to prove to them that you can solve their problem and that you can do it more effectively and efficiently than any other options that they might have—including doing nothing at all.

A good solution shows the prospect exactly how you will get results for them, and follows the format discussed in Chapter Five. Before getting into your solution, you might ask the prospect about their expectations. What kind of result would make this experience one of the best experiences of their career or life? What did they have in mind as an ideal coaching solution? What are their criteria in choosing whether or not to hire a coach? How much time are they willing to invest in a coaching engagement? How often would they like to meet, and over what time frame? The prospect might have answers or might not, but it is useful to start with their perspective and then build on it. That way, the prospect sees that you are personalizing a solution to their unique needs.

After you understand the client's expectations, it is time to present your solution at a high level and get their reaction. Here is your opportunity to show that you are confident and competent, and have a clear path to results. For instance:

"Joe, based on everything I've heard, and based on what has worked with other clients in similar situations, I have a three-part methodology that can solve your problem. First, I want to take a bit of time to assess the situation in more depth. This includes some one-on-one discussions with you, a ProfileXT assessment, and a 360-degree verbal assessment done confidentially with your team. We will also set specific goals to track progress throughout the coaching engagement. Based on the results of this process, we move to the second phase. Here, we will meet weekly for six months and work together to achieve the goals we set in Phase One. There are a variety of coaching tools we will use, including a simple behavioral coaching process and some role-play. By the end of six months, you should have achieved the goals we have set, and can move into Phase Three. Here, we meet monthly for six more months to make sure that the results are sustainable, and to address any setbacks that might come up."

In the above example, it would be helpful to include a graphic showing this methodology. I have found that it works best to draw your methodology from scratch while meeting with the client. It can be on a flip chart or just a plain piece of paper. I know one coach who even does this on a napkin during a lunch meeting. That way, you are spontaneous and can make any on-the-spot adjustments to address the prospect's specific issues.

You can also tell a few stories about the results you have gotten using this approach with others, as a form of proof.

Finally, ask the client for their advice about this approach. What concerns do they have? What do they like about it? What would they change?

QUESTION THREE: DO YOU WANT TO WORK WITH THEM?

There is one other question to answer before moving forward with a prospect: Do you want to work with them? Sometimes coaches get hired for the wrong reasons. I've had some clients who hired me more as a status symbol than to make changes in their lives. It's done in much the same way that some people love to brag about their psychiatrist. Similarly, some companies hire coaches and force them onto their managers, even if the managers are not open to being coached. Beyond these issues, you might meet with prospects who have questionable values, will be stingy with referrals, or that just rub you the wrong way.

You should have a set of criteria about the clients you like to work with. If you meet a prospect who doesn't fit enough of these criteria, refer them to a competitor!

Here are some examples:

- Are they even coachable? If you get a sense that your prospect isn't going to be open to coaching, won't do his assignments, and will constantly push back, you might be setting yourself up for lots of frustration if you let them become a client.

- What's the minimum size and length of an initial coaching engagement you are willing to accept?

- What are the opportunities for long-term revenues from this client? How much add-on work do you expect?

- What are the prospect's core values? Are they aligned with your values?

- Will the engagement give you the opportunity to create a new coaching process or product?

- Does the engagement fit with your capabilities and what you do best?

- Will the prospect stretch you so that you become a better coach?

- Can you do this in your sleep? If so, maybe it is time to upgrade your clients and the type of work you do.

- Will the prospect respect boundaries? For instance, you can tell even before they sign up whether a prospect is likely to call you at all hours for unscheduled support. Typically, this kind of prospect will argue with you when you contract with them. Beware! I had one client whom I knew would do this and took him on anyway. He traveled the world and had no respect for my time zone, calling me as late as 2 am. I had to reset boundaries with him, and he continued to violate them anyway. I raised my fees to a ridiculous level, hoping he would balk, and he accepted. Eventually I had to terminate the relationship.

- Will the prospect be stingy or generous with referrals? If you don't know, ask up front.

- Is this a high-profile client who will get you great publicity and add to your reputation?

- If things go wrong, is this the type of person who will sue you or go out of his way to hurt your reputation?

Sometimes you can go through the above questions with a prospect in a single meeting, and they become a client. Sometimes the fit is clear, the connection is there, and both coach and client can't wait to get started. Other times, the coach and prospect need more time to confirm fit and decide on a solution. There is no formula that says how long the process will take. However, if you get a sense that the above questions are not going to be answered with a resounding "yes," be wary. Ask tough questions early on, and be ready to move on to prospects who are more promising.

Chapter Seventeen

HANDLE CONCERNS AND OBJECTIONS WITH FINESSE AND GRACE

T he last chapter described the three questions that must be discussed with prospects to engage them and confirm a good fit. If you can answer all three of these questions with prospects, while also engaging them authentically, you have a good chance of gaining a new client. However, most prospects still have concerns and objections, and you need to address these before you can close the deal.

Now, a few coaches report that they have some sort of X factor that causes people to want to hire them right on the spot. They have some ethereal quality—maybe charisma, maybe a command of the laws of attraction, or maybe an incredible presence—that causes people to say, "I want you to coach me now." If you are in this category, congratulations! You have a rare and wonderful gift. However, if you don't have this superpower, don't get sucked into weekend seminars that claim to teach this ability to you. Instead, join the rest of us normal humans, and get used to handling prospect concerns and objections.

It is natural for prospects to have concerns before they hire you. Coaching requires mutual trust. Your coaching clients share sensitive issues and information with you, and most people are not comfortable doing that. Before someone hires you, he or she has to overcome skepticism, distrust, and even a bit of fear.

THREE TYPES OF PROSPECTS, AND THREE ATTITUDES FOR HANDLING OBJECTIONS.

There are three types of prospects when it comes to concerns and objections. First, some prospects have very legitimate objections that you must address before they sign on as a client. The second group wants to get started, but needs reassurance that coaching is the right thing for them and that you are the right coach. These types of prospects might ask the same question a few times, because they want to know they are making a wise, safe decision. The third group of prospects is the most frustrating. The people in this group could drive you crazy with all of their concerns and requests for information, probably want free coaching from you, and may never hire you anyway.

Three attitudes enable you to figure out which prospects are worth your time, and which are wasting it. First, be patient. It takes time to build trust. Prospects hire you at their pace, not yours. If you come across as impatient, using cheesy sales tactics, or being too pushy, they will run the other way. Give them the time they need to explore whether coaching is right for them. You can still ask questions to help them make a decision sooner rather than later, but ultimately they have to decide at their pace.

Second, be on equal ground with your prospects. Otherwise, they won't respect you. Nobody hires a coach whom they don't respect. You should feel 100 percent entitled to be open and authentic with prospects. If they say something that raises a red flag and makes you worry about the success of the relationship, you can and should address it there and then. For instance, if a prospect doesn't seem engaged and excited, tell him about your concern, just like you would to a client. Otherwise, you'll be chasing your prospects for what seems like forever, and feeling frustrated while they hem and haw, and ultimately never become a client.

Similarly, if the prospect keeps asking for more information, more meetings, and more proposals, be willing to ask for something in return. At the very least, get him to tell you what he will do with it by saying, "I can do that, but what happens next?" Alternatively, if the requests don't seem valid, but rather like ways to avoid signing up, tell the prospect that. Your time is valuable, too. For instance, when a prospect asks me for a brochure, I say, "I stopped printing brochures because I found that prospects who wanted brochures just wanted to read about coaching and not actually commit."

A great metaphor for this mindset comes from the movie *The Wizard of Oz*. The Wizard of Oz could have sent Dorothy home to Kansas and also helped her three friends when they first came to him. Instead, he asks them to go get the broom of the Wicked Witch of the West. He does this because he knows that they will give up or die trying. Nevertheless, Dorothy and her team risk everything to get that broom. Then, when they bring it back to him triumphantly, the Wizard tells them to go away again. This is when Toto pulls the curtain back and reveals the real wizard—a regular man. Now Dorothy is on equal footing with the wizard, and the wizard knows it. He finally helps Dorothy and her friends to get what they want.

As coaches, we have to watch out for requests to go and get the witch's broom. We need to stand our ground and realize that our prospects are regular people and not wizards. Once we do, we can handle their objections in ways that show whether they are serious about hiring us or not, as examples later in this chapter show.

The third mindset to have is a willingness to let prospects go if the fit isn't there. Prospects who say yes are great because you get a new client. As almost any sales training teaches, prospects who say no are great, too, because you can move on to more likely candidates and not waste your time. It's the prospects in the middle who rob you of your time, and you can never get lost time back. These are the prospects whom you have to manage. At some point, you have to realize that, if you have to push a prospect into a coaching relationship with you, you care more about their goals and aspirations than they do. It is better to move on. What's fascinating is that, when you do, some of these same prospects often come right back to you and sign up. It's just like the cliché advises, "When you love someone, let them go…." To see this for yourself, you have to be willing to let prospects go when they don't seem serious, won't make up their mind, or the fit isn't quite there.

THE OBJECTIONS TESTING LABORATORY.

Part Two of this book advised you to set up a testing laboratory for your business development activities. You should do the same thing when it comes to handling objections and concerns. That way, you keep improving your ability to handle the top objections that you encounter.

After you meet with a prospect, take some notes about the objections they raised, and how you addressed them. What worked? What will you try next time? As you work with more and more prospects, figure out the best response to each of the most common objections you get. That way, you take the awkwardness out of this part of the process, and can take advantage of the most efficient way to convert the most prospects to clients that you can, without wasting time on the ones who aren't ever going to hire you.

Use the table below as a template for your own objections testing laboratory:

Objections Notebook:

Objection	Current Best Response	New Response to Try Next Time	Notes/Results

TOP STRATEGIES TO HANDLE CONCERNS AND OBJECTIONS.

Following are some of the top strategies to handle concerns and objections from prospects. Try these and see which work for you, and in which situations.

Use your natural coaching skills to ask questions that get at the root concern; then address it authentically.

One skill that sets coaches apart is the ability to ask powerful, probing questions. This same skill serves us very well when prospects have concerns and objections. When a prospect raises a concern, don't jump to answer. Don't try to read the prospect's mind and guess why he raised the concern. If you do, you might raise more serious issues in the prospect's mind. Instead, ask questions. Keep asking until you get at the real concern or realize that the prospect didn't have a serious issue but was just curious about something. Then, if there is a real concern, you know what it is, you can empathize with the prospect, and you can answer the real issue directly and authentically.

Ask the prospect for their advice about how to resolve the issue.

When the prospect raises an issue, ask what they would need as a solution to the issue in order to move forward. For instance, if they tell you that one hour a week is not enough, ask how much time would work for them. This is another standard coaching conversation, one that guides the prospect to solve the issue on their own. Then you can decide whether the prospect's resolution works for you and either move forward or provide an alternative idea. That way, you and the prospect work together to design the engagement.

Turn negatives into positives and vice versa.

I've yet to meet a coach who didn't have some insecurity about his credentials, experience, and validity. Sometimes I wonder if almost every coach doesn't feel like a big fraud inside. Are you too young? Too old? Don't have the right or enough credentials? Have so many credentials that you are perceived to be too academic? Have too little experience? Don't have a Ph.D. in psychology? Are too much of a generalist? Are too much of a specialist? Are you a woman in a man's industry? Are you a man, and worry that men won't open up to another man? We all have strengths and weaknesses. The key is to turn our weaknesses into perceived strengths. If a prospect suggests you are too young, turn that into a plus: "Yes, and that means I see things from a very different, fresh perspective." If a prospect raises the fact that you don't have an MBA, that's great: "Yes, you have the MBA, and so does everyone on your management team. I bring an entirely different way of thinking and set of experiences to the table. My methodology will show you insights into success that MBA programs don't teach."

Revisit past conversations about how serious the problem is and what it is costing.

If the prospect seems to be wavering, go back to the questions you already should have asked about the costs of the problem. For instance, "Last time we spoke, you gave me many reasons why this problem is hurting your fulfillment and productivity. Is that problem still there, or has something changed?" This strategy allows you to get back to the pain the prospect feels. From there, you can ask more questions to reconfirm the value of your solutions. Essentially, you recreate a context that reminds the prospect why he can benefit from coaching and get the conversation back on track.

Give something only when you get something in return.

For instance, if the prospect wants you to have yet another meeting with him, agree—but only if he agrees to have all relevant decision makers at the meeting and to make a decision whether or not to hire you within 30 minutes of that meeting. If the prospect asks for more time to make a decision, ask for a specific deadline, a date when you can expect his decision. If he still hasn't made up his mind by that date, be ready to move on. Perhaps call him to remind them that he promised to make a decision and didn't get back to you. Tell him that you assume this means they aren't moving forward, but you just wanted to confirm before you moved on. This gives the prospect one final chance to move forward. If he doesn't, let it go and find another prospect.

Suggest that perhaps there isn't a fit, and observe how they react.

If you get the sense that the prospect isn't serious about hiring you, tell him. Then let him react. He will either reveal that he is more serious than you thought and just need some little thing to move forward, or that he isn't serious and you can both move on. At a minimum, you have let him know that you aren't afraid to raise tough issues and are worthy of respect.

Get creative with terms.

Sometimes the issue comes down to the details of closing the deal. If the prospect can only sign a check for $10,000 without going to his boss, but you wanted a $20,000 engagement, figure out a way to do a $10,000 engagement and get hired on the spot. If the prospect's budget cycle starts in two months, find a way to get him to sign up now and pay once the budget cycle begins.

Provide an "if, then" statement when they want assurances.

Some prospects object to hiring you because they want a guarantee of results. It is hard to give an ironclad guarantee in coaching, because so much depends on the client. If you don't have the authority to act or make decisions, how can you guarantee results? You can't. What you can do is frame your guarantee in "If, then" terms: "If you do your coaching homework, if you come to each session and give it your best, and if you are willing to get outside your comfort zone from time to time, then yes—you will get the results you seek."

Reframe.

Coaches are skilled at helping clients reframe limiting beliefs. Use this same skill with prospect objections. For instance, if a prospect tells you that your prices are expensive, reframe the way they perceive your fees. There are a few ways to do that. First: "Joe, my fees are a fraction of the value of the results you said you wanted to achieve. To be precise, they are 1/20th of the value. What investments do you have that are giving you a 20 times return on investment in a year's time?" Second: "Mary, my fees are nothing compared to a consulting firm like McKinsey." Third: "Steve, you told me you want to get in shape so you can be alive when your newborn baby has her wedding. Are you sure my fees aren't worth that?" Similarly, let's say the prospect objects to paying so much money for a few hours a month. Reframe by replying, "Your time is valuable. I can spend as much time with you as you want, but wouldn't you rather get results in less time?"

Reassure.

If your prospect repeats the same questions, he might not be bringing up an objection. It's more likely that he is simply looking for reassurance. People want to know that everything is going to be okay. Tell him that you would really like to work with him, and give him authentic reasons why. Empathize with his issues, while letting him know that there really is a way to make things better.

Say less and get more.

Sometimes we derail a sale by talking too much. If your prospect has a question, get to the reason behind the question; answer his question, and then stop. Be careful about providing more information than the prospect requested. If you do, you might end up raising even more concerns and issues.

Let the prospect work it out.

Sometimes the best way to handle a concern is by agreeing with the client, or keeping quiet and letting the prospect work it out on his own. For instance, if the prospect says, "This is expensive," you might simply nod and then keep quiet. He might just be working through the issues in his head, and not actually raising an objection. If he keeps raising the issue, you can ask questions to understand more about it and how to resolve it together.

Remember that the above approaches only work when you remain authentic, open, and honest. The instant you start to sound like a salesperson, you sacrifice trust. Also, you shouldn't have to feel like you are selling your coaching services, or pushing them onto the prospect. A prospect wants to make up his own mind on his own time, and doesn't want to feel pressure. Make sure he is committed to the process, too. When I feel like a prospect is making me do all the work during the selling process, it raises a big red flag for me, and I say, "I feel like I have to sell this to you. That means I care more about your goals than you do, and that's not going to make for a productive coaching relationship." Then I keep quiet and listen to what the prospect has to say. If they don't show more interest and commitment, I move on.

LIST YOUR TOP TEN OBJECTIONS AND HOW YOU HANDLE THEM.

Take a few moments now to list the most common objections you get from prospects. Write down your best approach to handle them. That way, you have your testing lab in place for logging objections and can make your selling process more systematic.

Your Top Ten Objections from Prospects	Your Best Current Strategy to Handle Each Objection

Chapter Eighteen

STRATEGIES TO CLOSE THE DEAL

Y ou can't push someone into a coaching engagement. However, there are some simple, natural conversations you can have to drive prospects towards a decision. This chapter suggests nine ways to take that final step from having a prospect to having a client.

ONE: ASK "WHAT DO YOU WANT TO DO NEXT?"

This is one of the most powerful questions you can ask to assess where a prospect is and whether he is ready to hire you. If he replies, "Let's start," then you are in business. If not, his response tells you where he stands and what he needs to move forward. This gives you a chance to handle his concerns, and even set a deadline by which he will decide.

TWO: TELL THEM THAT YOU ARE EXCITED
TO WORK WITH THEM AND GET STARTED.

Your own enthusiasm for the prospect and the engagement is sometimes enough to get you hired. For instance, "Steve, I've really enjoyed talking to you about the challenges you face leading this organization, and about the opportunities you have to grow the company. I also like your leadership style and admire your willingness to take risk. I would love to have a coaching relationship with you, and I sincerely hope that you agree."

THREE: CREATE URGENCY.

If the prospect is wavering, remind him of the issues and how serious they are. In consulting lingo, you have to create a burning platform for the client. This is now a decades-old term, but it's still a useful one. Imagine that your client is standing on a very high platform, with no way down except to jump. Of course, the client doesn't want to jump. You have to convince the prospect that the platform is burning and that the pain of staying on the platform is much worse than the pain that will come from jumping.

To create a burning platform, ask the prospect yet more questions to review and perhaps uncover even more costs and emotional pain related to his problem. Ask what will happen if he doesn't do anything about the issues now, in a month, in three months, or within six months. Ask for permission to give your own reasons about why the prospect should move forward, and then hit him hard with a great case for change.

FOUR: THROW THEM A LIFELINE.

Have you ever felt frustrated because you knew you could help the prospect with your coaching, but he was just too wrapped up in his own mess to see it? With some prospects, it's as if they were stuck in quicksand. All they can see is the quicksand, so they keep clutching at it, hoping that they can flail their way out. Of course, that only makes things worse. Meanwhile, you are standing on the side of the quicksand, holding a rope that will save the prospect. All he has to do is grab it, but he can't or won't look up and see this. He is too focused on the immediate crisis to take even a second to accept your help.

In these cases, take a stand for the client. Tell them how you feel: "Jim, you've said that you are burning out working 90 hours a week. I've shown you that I have a time management and coaching process that can get you to a manageable week. It can get you your family and free time back, and that can help you get back into a healthy lifestyle. But for some reason you won't listen. Everything you've done so far only causes you to work even longer hours. Can I ask you to take a leap of faith? I know I can help you, and it frustrates me that you can't or won't listen. Please. I want to work with you. I know my coaching system will work for you. Take the lifeline I am offering...."

FIVE: SHOW EMPATHY.

A soft way to close is by saying, "Margaret, if I were in your shoes, I would move forward with our coaching relationship. You've told me that you are frustrated with the results you are getting with your team and are at your wits' end. If I were in your shoes, I would definitely invest an hour a week with a coach who has a methodology like the one I've shared with you. I don't see any downside, and the upside is huge. Of course, I'm not in your shoes. What do you think?"

SIX: AGREE TO A DEADLINE.

If you have a prospect who wavers or keeps asking for more information, at least get him to commit to a deadline for making a decision. If the deadline passes and he hasn't hired you, find out why, and be prepared to move on.

SEVEN: REDUCE THE SCOPE.

The prospect might not be ready to hire you for a large-scale coaching engagement. However, they might be ready to hire you for an assessment or a short coaching relationship to test you out. Suggest some options so that you can at least get your foot in the door and show what you can do.

EIGHT: SUGGEST THERE ISN'T A FIT AND BE PREPARED TO MOVE ON.

Finally, if you have a prospect who won't move forward no matter what you try, be blunt. Tell him that you don't know what is going on or why he won't be honest with you, but that it seems clear that he doesn't want to move forward. You might even suggest some reasons that you think are causing the indecision. Include your concern that he is too polite to tell you that he isn't interested, or that he isn't as serious about solving his problem as he claims. Then listen to the response and go from there. If the prospect continues to hem and haw, but won't follow through, you should realize that he isn't a real prospect—at least not right now. Don't be obnoxious when you do this. Don't burn bridges. Leave the door open in case the prospect changes his mind. Put a note in your calendar to follow up in a few months. However, now you can spend your time working with more qualified prospects, getting more visible in your target market, and delighting actual clients with great results.

NINE: BE PATIENT.

You never know. Sometimes, long after you have given up, a prospect might call you and tell you he is ready to hire you. As Deborah Burgesser of Executive Steps LLC shares, "Relationship development with prospective clients is key, and can take as little as a few hours to a few days, a few months, and even a few years. I have a new client who has been a prospective client for three years. He faces the same pains today that he was facing three years ago. It just took three years for him to finally throw up his hands and say, 'I need a business coach.' My persistent interest in him and his business paid off."

Chapter Nineteen

HOW TO WRITE A POWERFUL PROPOSAL—AND WHEN NOT TO.

When a prospect asks you for a proposal, do you immediately think, "Yes! I am definitely going to get hired!"? If you do, you might be fooling yourself. Often prospects ask for proposals because they are too polite to tell you to buzz off. This causes many coaches to spend hours and hours on a proposal that the prospect is only going to throw away, while requesting more information or saying, "I need more time to think about it."

The fact is that you can't read the prospect's mind about budget, scope, goals, and boundaries. You can only insert that information into a proposal when the prospect has already agreed to the crucial elements of a coaching engagement. Once that happens, you are ready to write a proposal—and the proposal really becomes a contract ready for the prospect to sign.

Therefore, when a prospect asks for a proposal before committing to the terms of a formal coaching relationship, here is what you say: "That's great news, and I thank you. However, I can't write a proposal until we both agree on all of the terms of our coaching engagement. Otherwise, I'm just guessing and trying to read your mind about what you want. My time is valuable, as is yours. For that reason alone, I don't write proposals unless the client agrees to move forward. That way, the proposal simply confirms that we both are on the same page and ready to start. Are you ready to move forward…?"

Assuming the prospect says yes, you can start confirming the details of your coaching relationship, starting with fees, how long the initial coaching agreement lasts, how often you meet, and when you start.

If, as you craft the proposal together, the prospect balks at any of the points you make, then you know you have more work to do before you get hired. For instance, if they won't agree to the budget you propose, you know that you have to revisit the value the prospect expects to get from the coaching relationship, or propose a smaller scope. If the prospect still balks, it might be because he really doesn't have the money to hire you—regardless of what he said earlier on in the process—and you have to discover what has changed.

A good coaching proposal contains the following elements:

OPENING.

See the sample at the end of this chapter for an example of some introductory sentences to get the proposal started. Tell the prospect how excited you are to move forward, and remind him of the date when you will start the engagement.

BACKGROUND.

This is the most important part of the proposal. You have to capture the issues the prospect faces and what they are costing him. This is crucial, because it reminds the prospect of the value he can expect from the coaching relationship.

GOALS.

Make sure that both you and the prospect agree on the outcomes and goals that will make the coaching relationship worthwhile and valuable.

APPROACH.

How will you go about solving the prospect's problem?

SCOPE OF DISCUSSIONS.

What do you discuss during coaching sessions, and what don't you discuss? For instance, I am an executive and business coach. I don't mind listening to clients when they discuss issues with their marriage and kids, but that's not my area of expertise, and I make that clear up front.

FEES.

Quote your fees and payment terms here. For instance, I quote my fees on a per-engagement basis. But in this section of the proposal, I break them down on a monthly basis so that they appear smaller.

TERMINATION.

What is your policy about termination? I try to make my contracts ironclad, with no termination. I don't want clients who feel like they have a way out. I want clients who are fully engaged and committed—clients who know that there is nowhere to hide except by moving forward and past tough issues.

CLIENT RESPONSIBILITIES.

Describe what you need from the client for the coaching relationship to be successful. See the list in the sample proposal at the end of this chapter.

SIGNATURES AND DATE.

Don't forget to sign the proposal.

Note that the above elements, and the example that follows, probably won't satisfy your attorney or your prospect's corporate counsel if you are coaching an executive or manager. Get legal advice as appropriate for your situation and risk tolerance, and adjust the proposal/contract to meet the needs of the specific situation and client requirements. In my case, I take time to build trust with my clients, so much so that a handshake is almost enough. That makes proposal/contract writing much easier. I've never been sued, and I've never had to sue. If a conflict comes up, my relationship with the client is strong enough that we can work together to resolve the matter, without having to resort to lawyers.

SAMPLE PROPOSAL:

Joe:

Thank you for your interest in a coaching engagement to help you clarify the future direction of your organization. I am excited to work with you! This proposal confirms our discussion and agreement. If it accurately captures what you and I discussed, please sign and return it to me, and I will do the same with a duplicate. Per our discussion, we will begin with a session on Monday, June 4, at 10 am.

Background

Your training and development business has grown to the point where you are achieving ambitious financial goals. However, you are traveling every weekend and realize that your current operating model is not sustainable given your personal goals. You would like to take the business in a new direction in order to work less and yet make even more money. You have a number of ideas to do that, including developing what you call "clones" of yourself, but you would like coaching to flesh out those ideas, decide on a direction, and create a formal operating/action plan to make your ideas happen. Finally, you are concerned about how to go about building leverage in your company, as in the past you have shown a "lack of interest and talent" (your words!) in managing others. In fact, you have experienced high turnover among the staff that you currently have, and want to get to the bottom of the behaviors and issues causing this turnover.

Goals

To that end, you have the following goals you want to achieve through coaching:

1. Implement ways to create leverage in your business, which will allow you to make more money with less time and travel.

2. Make decisions about a number of ideas you have to grow your business.

3. Drill down to a specific operating model, so that your business essentially runs without you.

4. Handle the issue you raised about your own strengths and weaknesses so that they don't get in the way of creating leverage. Specifically, you acknowledge that you are a visionary and are extremely strong at making high-level business contacts. However, you have never had success managing other people, and you don't particularly enjoy that aspect of running a business.

Approach

You have asked me to provide coaching and mentoring to help you achieve the above goals.

The coaching process will take place during a 55-minute phone conversation weekly, and also in between sessions via email to review any homework. You have agreed to a six-month commitment, after which time we will review where we are and determine how or whether to continue the coaching process.

The coaching process will include the following elements in addition to our actual coaching conversations: creating an overall plan of attack or coaching plan, and getting your agreement that the plan makes sense; confirming desired goals and approach before each meeting; assessing your satisfaction and the results you are getting after each meeting and every month during the process; and giving and receiving feedback from one another to make sure that the program is providing you with outstanding value.

In parallel with these coaching sessions, I will conduct a 360-degree assessment with up to 15 people with whom you currently work, and have worked with in the past. This assessment will consist of a face-to-face interview with people inside and outside your organization who know you best, including some clients. That way, we can collect objective data about how others perceive you and opportunities for you to improve your effectiveness. To maintain a safe environment, the assessment will not share specific comments made by individuals without their permission, and will instead look for more general trends.

Scope of Discussions

Per our discussions, you are comfortable having conversations about your business, working with current employees and contractors, and your own strengths and perceived weaknesses as a manager. You are open to exploring your perceptions, behaviors, and feelings as the CEO of your company.

You also give permission for me to speak to up to 15 people, including former and current employees and clients, on a confidential basis to get data about how others perceive you. We will discuss the general trends, but not what specific people said.

If our coaching sessions begin to discuss other aspects of your life (e.g., marriage, fatherhood, health and wellness), you understand that—beyond a certain level of inquiry—these domains are not my area of expertise and that you may need to see another expert.

Fees

The fees, for this six-month coaching program, are $2,500 per month, 50% payable with the signing of this agreement and 50% after three months.

Please make checks payable to [COMPANY NAME] and mail to [ADDRESS].

Termination

You have acknowledged that the coaching process requires commitment and the understanding that issues might come up that will make you feel uncomfortable.

For this reason, this contract may not be terminated. No refunds are issued.

Your Responsibilities

You agree to the following:

1. The coaching relationship is important to you, and you are committed to achieving the goals outlined above.

2. You will attend all coaching sessions on time.

3. If you need to reschedule a coaching session, you will do so with at least 72 hours' notice. Otherwise, I am under no obligation to make up that session.

4. During coaching sessions, you will be present, with no external distractions (cell phones, other people, email, etc.).

5. You will complete any assignments that you agree to do, on time.

6. You will be open and honest during the sessions, which includes giving advice to me about how you can get more value from sessions.

7. The agreement we have includes weekly sessions and email. It does not include unscheduled calls or calls after business hours.

8. You understand that my business relies on referrals. Therefore, you agree that, as you get value from our work together, you will sit down with me to discuss other people you know who might find value from my services.

Joe, I am excited about working with you and helping you take your business to its next phase of growth. Please sign below to indicate that you accept the above terms.

Sincerely,

[YOUR NAME]

Step IV

KEEP CLIENTS FOR LIFE, OR AT LEAST FOR A LONG TIME

The best source of revenue for a coach is almost always current clients. The most successful coaches understand the value of the first client, and every client that follows. They understand what it means to deliver value and create raving fans. Finally, they are diligent when it comes to anticipating client needs and finding new ways to serve them, as well as other people in their organization, professional network, or life.

Chapter Twenty

THE VALUE OF YOUR FIRST CLIENT, AND EVERY CLIENT WHO FOLLOWS

I f you are starting out as a coach, keep learning, testing, and moving forward until you get your first client. Once you get the first client, things start to get easier. You have more confidence, and realize that—if you can get that one first client—you can fill your practice. Prospects are more likely to become clients, because you can share real results with them, and they see that you have a real practice. Best of all, your first client becomes a source of referrals and introductions for you. They will open up a whole new, extremely powerful marketing source that was not available to you before.

Meanwhile, if you have an existing practice, never forget the value of even a single client. Coaches get so enamored with the thrill of landing new clients that they sometimes forget the value of their existing clients. Every single client is a potential source of revenue from ongoing engagements, potential referrals, and opportunities to take what you have learned from your work together and turn it into a new coaching program or product.

The specific, measurable lifetime value of a client is not hard to calculate:

1. (Value of your average engagement with a client) X (Number of engagements over the lifetime of the client) = Direct value of a client

2. (Referrals from that client) X (Direct value of a client) = Value from the client in referrals

3. 1 + 2 = Lifetime value of a client

For instance, suppose that you are an executive coach and earn $25,000 for a one-year client engagement. Suppose further that a single client tends to last, on average, five years. The direct value of that client is $25,000 X 5, or $125,000.

Now assume that every client gives you at least three referrals to new clients, whether in their own organization or elsewhere. That adds an addition $125,000 X 3, or $375,000 to the value of that client.

In this example, a single client is worth $125,000 plus $375,000 in referrals, or $500,000. The lifetime value of a client to you may be higher or lower, depending on your target market and whether or not you have low-pricing self-esteem. Regardless, take a moment and estimate the lifetime value of a client in your coaching practice.

Meanwhile, as the infomercial says, "That's not all!" You also should add the following less-easily quantifiable benefits that every client brings to you:

- The increase in your reputation by having that client as part of your client roster.

- The value of having an added testimonial.

- The value of having an added case study.

- The value of getting additional introductions that the client makes for you, even if they don't directly result in new clients.

- The value of what you learn from that client and how it makes you a better coach and expert.

- The value of any ancillary products or services you are able to create based on work with that client, such as a new coaching methodology, a new information product, or a new group-coaching program.

As you grow your practice, keep track of what a single client is worth to you, and keep trying to improve that value. Raise your fees per engagement. Increase how long a typical client stays with you. Add more services that they can buy from you, like facilitated retreats, trainings, and group coaching programs. Get more referrals from each client. Learn as much as you can from each client engagement and productize it so that you create more intellectual capital for your professional practice.

At the same time, track the clients who come from each client the way that you would track a family tree from a single ancestor. I did this exercise five years after I started coaching clients in the non-profit sector. I was amazed to discover that about half of my then-current clients came from my very first client in that market. Here is how the value unfolded in my case:

- After doing a free seminar, the executive director of a small non-profit hired me to help him be a more effective leader in his organization.

- He then brought me in to work with his Board of Directors, for some board development and strategic planning work.

- A member of the Board of Directors was serving on another non-profit and asked me to work with the executive director and Board of that organization.

- That same process led to work with three more non-profits in the area.

- One of those executive directors was a leader in the local non-profit support center. He helped me get hired by that support center to do research about how non-profit leaders develop their leadership and management skills, and common trends in leadership development and needs. This project got me in front of 50 non-profit and community leaders, and led to my presenting my findings to the board of directors of the non-profit support center. Much more work followed from the connection I made on this project.

- Based on the above work, the executive director of a billion-dollar foundation contacted me to work with him and his Board of Directors on grant-making priorities. I worked with them for a number of years, and got many more referrals to clients based on my connection to that foundation.

- The bookkeeper of my first non-profit client did some bookkeeping work with another non-profit, and told the executive director there about me. He engaged me to be a coach and organizational development consultant for a consortium of university professors and administrators that had received $80 million in National Science Foundation Funding. They needed help learning how to form an organization and work together as a team.

- One member of the consortium brought me into her university to coach her and other faculty about how to collaborate more effectively.

- In addition, my work with that consortium got me introduced to some administrators at the National Science Foundation. They referred me to the leaders of another consortium that was applying for funding, and I got hired to be on their team as a coach and consultant.

- One of the members of that consortium brought me into his university, where I became his coach. He then referred me to a colleague in the university, and I became his coach. When he moved to a new unit in the university, he introduced me to his boss, and I became his coach.

- One of my clients at this same university referred me to his wife, who was running a non-profit and needed a coach. She hired me.

- That very first client moved on to start a very successful for-profit company, and hired me as a coach to help him be a better CEO and build his company so that it was less reliant on him. The chain continued to grow from there...

The total amount the first client paid me over this time was not more than $25,000. However, the stream of business I got based on that first client dwarfs that amount. It has to be at least in the high six figures.

The lesson is clear: Never forget the value of your first client, and every client thereafter.

Chapter Twenty-One

DELIVER VALUE AND CREATE RAVING FANS

he last chapter used the analogy of the family tree to describe the value of a single client. Another useful image for this value comes from a natural phenomenon called a tidal bore. A tidal bore occurs when an incoming tide goes into a narrow channel, like a river, and creates a very long wave. As I write this, a couple of paddle surfers are in the news because they recently rode a tidal bore in Alaska for five miles! Think of each and every client as a potentially very long wave. Then give them so much value that they let you ride that wave for a long, long time. That way, you get an ongoing stream of work and referrals.

There are some simple but hard-hitting questions to ask yourself to know whether you deliver value to your clients and have raving fans:

- How long does your typical client relationship last? If your average client engages you for less than three years, you might not be bringing enough value to your coaching relationships. The top coaches with whom I've worked report that their average client relationship lasts five years, with some clients staying with them for more than a decade! There should always be something else to work on with your clients to help them continue to develop and get great results.

- How many referrals and introductions does each client send your way, whether you ask them to or not? If you get fewer than two referrals from your average client, they may not see enough value in what you do to rave about you to others. Two referrals is a minimum. If you really turn clients into raving fans, and you make requesting referrals a habit, you should get many more than that from each client.

- What percentage of your clients provide you with glowing testimonials when you ask? At least 85 percent of your clients should be willing to do this.

- Do your clients see enough value in your expertise that they call you before they make any major decision? A business coach I know insists that his coaching clients don't make any significant business decisions, investments, or purchases without calling him first. That's part of his coaching contract, and it reinforces his value to the client as a trusted advisor and member of his inner circle.

Achieving these benchmarks requires an understanding of value, which goes way beyond the basic competencies being promoted by various coaching associations. Following are eight areas where you need to excel in order to provide a total coaching experience that delights your clients.

ONE: EMBODY THE RIGHT ORIENTATIONS AS A COACH, SO THAT THE CLIENT EXPERIENCE OF YOU IS OUTSTANDING.

Top coaches have a set of orientations that enables them to connect with their clients on a deep professional and personal level. These orientations include:

- Taking a stand to help the client achieve his or her most ambitious aspirations.

- Being authentic, open, and honest, even if it feels difficult to tell the ugly truth.

- Demonstrating the highest levels of integrity, ethics, and professionalism.

- Having presence, focus, and grounding in every interaction with a client.

- Coming from a sense of service to the client.

- Being willing to be vulnerable, as opposed to coming across as a know-it-all guru.

- Being a source of possibility and opportunity, even when the client feels like giving up.

- Balancing outcomes and relationships so that the client doesn't feel coerced or inappropriately pushed towards results, and also doesn't feel like the coach avoids difficult conversations to preserve the relationship.

- Having the confidence that you are valuable to your clients, and the willingness to keep building your skills to support that confidence.

TWO: CREATE AN ENVIRONMENT WHERE AMAZING THINGS CAN OCCUR.

Clients don't need a coach to get the results, which would happen for them anyway. They want breakthroughs—new ways of being and doing that make incredible things happen, things that didn't seem possible before the coaching relationship began. Help create an environment where that can occur. For instance, before you start an engagement, ask, "What would you have to achieve to make this one of the most valuable experiences of your career or life?" Similarly, before every coaching session, remember to ask, "What's going to make this hour the best hour of your week?"

Follow up after each session, and periodically during the engagement. Ask the client whether or not he is creating amazing results through the coaching process. If he isn't, review the goals he had when he first started, and what needs to happen to get back on track.

Creating a context for amazing things to occur doesn't mean that you make false promises to the client. That will only frustrate both of you. Amazing doesn't always mean that the sky opens, angels start to sing, and peace suddenly fills the hearts of all people. Very small changes can be quite amazing, too, because the repercussions of those changes reach far and wide. For instance, I worked with a manager who was about to lose her job because she was dismissive to her employees. We made a few small, simple changes in the way she communicated, and it made all the difference. Morale improved. Turnover decreased. Her team exceeded their goals and felt great doing it.

Another piece of creating an environment for amazing things to occur is seeing your client as capable of doing amazing things in the first place. If we don't see our clients as amazing, then that will show up in our coaching. We let our clients quit on their true aspirations and goals. We need to see the potential that our clients have, and engage with them as who they can be, not who they are right now. Your clients will love you for this, because very few people in their lives, if anyone, see them this way or engage with them this way.

THREE: DEFINE RESULTS, GET RESULTS, AND ACKNOWLEDGE RESULTS.

A crucial part of bringing value is getting results. Before the engagement begins, set goals to define results for the client during your time together. Before every session with the client, set goals that define results during that session. Challenge the client to set a minimum goal that they are confident they can achieve, and a stretch goal that would be amazing to achieve. Figure out what's in the way of getting those results, and work with the client to handle them. Track the goals throughout the process and make mid-course corrections in your coaching as needed until the client gets results.

Finally, acknowledge the client for getting results—and have him acknowledge the results, too. Most people are harder on themselves than they need to be, and need a coach to make sure that they pat themselves on the back when they achieve. Also, by acknowledging results, your client also acknowledges your contributions to the coaching process.

FOUR: ASK ABOUT THE VALUE THE CLIENT IS GETTING.

Check in frequently to see what insights the client is having, and what value they are getting. Executive coach Len Rothman, President of Leadership @ Work, asks clients two questions at the end of every session: "What was the most valuable thing you got out of today's meeting?" and "What was the incremental value of today's meeting toward your long term goal?" That way, value is always in the foreground.

FIVE: GET ADVICE TO BE BETTER.

Did you know that many coaches think they are phenomenal at delivering value for their clients until—when an objective third party conducts confidential interviews with their clients—they learn that they aren't as great as they thought? It's true. I know this because I've interviewed clients on behalf of coaches and had to deliver this news to them.

Don't assume that you are delivering value to your clients simply because you have fancy coaching designations or thousands of coaching hours under your belt. Ask your clients. Have a periodic review of what they like and don't like about your coaching, and how they can get even more value from your relationship. Listen to their advice, and take it to heart.

At the same time, every year or so, have the courage to get a trusted colleague to interview your clients confidentially on your behalf. Try to get at least one piece of advice that will help you be a better coach.

Your clients will appreciate this for two reasons. First, it demonstrates a level of integrity and commitment to improvement that few other coaches have. Second, you will keep getting better, and your clients will notice.

SIX: MANAGE THE PROCESS.

Coaching is a process. Help your clients go through this process so that they trust you and feel confidence in what you are trying to do. Set up a formal coaching plan early on, so that they know where you are heading. At each and every session, quickly review where you have been, where you are today, and where you are going—and make sure the client agrees. At the end of every session, review what the client achieved, and what will happen next time. Before you do a specific exercise, like role-play or active inquiry, set it up so that the client knows what to expect and is at ease.

SEVEN: NURTURE THE RELATIONSHIP.

Coaching is not about getting through weekly or monthly meetings that have a start and an end. You are in a trusted, intimate relationship with your clients. To gain a client for life, you must nurture your relationship with him.

As the coaching relationship progresses, you learn more and more about each client's aspirations, interests, passions, likes, and dislikes. Help him achieve those aspirations, even if they are outside the scope of the coaching relationship. Send articles of interest. Subscribe to an executive book summary service like SoundView Executive Book Summaries, and share new books and ideas that might be of interest. Make introductions. Let him know about opportunities that might be of interest. Talk about common values and hobbies. Make him famous by helping him give speeches to his association, or by co-writing articles in the industry trade publications. If you feel it is appropriate, send him cards or small gifts to acknowledge important milestones for him.

EIGHT: IF VALUE STOPS, STOP THE COACHING RELATIONSHIP.

Some coaching clients, especially those who are especially desperate or vulnerable, can be manipulated into spending their last dollar with an unscrupulous coach. Don't ever take advantage of that kind of opportunity, or you'll hurt your reputation and the entire coaching industry.

For instance, I worked with the CEO of what was once a $12 million software integrator. The business had imploded, to the point that the CEO went from having a net worth in the millions to owing so much money that he could no longer pay the mortgage on the house he bought for his mother. I worked with him for a few months to try to help him to resuscitate the business. By the end, I realized I couldn't help him and—while he was open to a longer engagement—I refused to take any more of his money. I continued to help him and his management team as best I could on an informal basis, but he needed expertise that I couldn't provide, so I ended the business relationship. I know that I could have made more money from him, but I wouldn't have felt good about it, wouldn't have gotten results for him, and eventually my reputation would have suffered.

Again: If the client stops getting value, stop the coaching relationship. That way, they remember you as a high-integrity professional who isn't desperate for work. They will be more likely to serve as a reference, send you referrals, and hire you again when a new pressing problem comes up later.

Review the eight areas one more time. Where do you excel in delivering value and creating raving fans among your clients? Where could you do a better job?

Chapter Twenty-Two

FROM FOOTHOLD TO A MAJOR PRESENCE

A mentor taught me that you never try to get rich on the first engagement with a client. Instead, start small and build your presence over time. For instance, start with a single assessment or small coaching engagement with a manager or executive in a company. Then keep finding ways to bring that client value. As you do, find ways to get introductions to others in the organization so you can start working with them as well.

Of course, the best way to do this is by asking for referrals and introductions, using the process described in a previous practice. Following are other tactics to successfully go from having a foothold to a major presence with your clients:

ASSESSMENTS.

Assessments are a great way to start small and build up. A good assessment doesn't cost much and blows your clients away with insights about who they are. After completing an assessment, most clients should see opportunities to improve, and this leads to coaching engagements for you. Also, once your client's colleagues see the results of the assessment, they get curious about what their assessment profile might show.

An old-school approach that works very well is doing a 360-degree verbal assessment. In this process, you ask for feedback about your client from 10 to 15 colleagues up, down, and across the organization. Len Rothman, President of Leadership @ Work, uses the 360-degree process he learned from The Center for Executive Coaching. At the end of the 360 assessment, Len asks the interviewee, "What has been the value of our meeting to you?" Len thinks that because of that question, several interviewees have become clients and made sure to include a 360 assessment in their coaching engagement. This allows him to repeat the process. In one national organization, Len interviewed more than 75 percent of the organization's leadership, and 15 percent of those interviewees became clients. He has expanded his presence to the point where he has hired other coaches to do some of the work for him.

Off-the-shelf tools also work well. For instance, Michael Pacholek of Summit Assessment Solutions LLC is a self-proclaimed assessment junkie. He loves assessments, especially the Profiles International suite of tools. He shares his experience with assessments and how they help get executive coaching engagements:

As executive coaches, it's important that we know and understand our clients better than they understand themselves by utilizing a quantifiable information source to look at the total person. The client needs to have really good self-recognition of their strengths and how to utilize those strengths in their current or future roles. The ProfileXT assessment allows us to use information to competitive advantage in the coaching relationship by providing an understanding of the following:

- *Thinking Style: How the person processes and retains information, which enables us to adjust our coaching to their preferences in learning and communicating with others.*

- *Behavior Traits: Allows us to learn the client's core competencies and strengths in relationship to the rest of the working population and their current or future roles.*

- *Occupational Interest: Provides insight into what types of activities will engage and motivate the client in the coaching relationship.*

This information is then combined into a one-hour executive session that allows the coach and the individual to have an open, honest conversation that focuses on the strengths of the individual. Providing someone with the opportunity to talk about themselves, their strengths, and their interactions with others allows the coach to establish a much higher degree of trust, credibility, and rapport with the individual. Think about it—when was the last time you were given an opportunity to talk about yourself for an hour? This increases the opportunity to achieve results at a much quicker pace than would be possible without the use of the ProfileXT assessment. It is important to note that the executive session can be used to pre-qualify candidates or once you have entered into the coaching relationship.

However, be careful of using the saturated and superficial assessments that are on the market. There are many of them, and they won't set you apart.

Michael offers insights about this problem, too: *Executive Coaches need to hold themselves to a higher standard by using assessment tools that have up-to-date validation studies and reliability coefficients that meet or exceed Department of Labor Guidelines. Coaches should also have knowledge about the differences between an ipsative assessment vs. a normative assessment and their appropriate uses. For more information, visit the Department of Labor website and get their publication about thirteen principles for using assessments.*

FROM COACHING A CLIENT TO COACHING HIS TEAM.

When you work with a client, look for opportunities to coach his management team. This is a fairly easy transition to make. At some point, your client will say, "I'm doing all of this work on me, but my team still has their own issues." That's the opening for you to start coaching his team, too. You can offer to coach specific individuals, or do group coaching, or a combination of both.

FOLLOW THE CLIENT AS HE MOVES UP, ACROSS, AND OUT.

In our volatile economy, it is unlikely that your client will remain in the same place into the long term. They might get promoted, make a lateral move to another unit, or leave the company altogether and find another opportunity. All of these present opportunities for you to keep your presence where the client had been, and develop a new presence where the client is heading. For instance, my clients in university settings tend to move around a lot. I followed one client from a small research organization within the university, to a major academic department, to an outreach group, and finally to a group commercializing technology. Each move brought new coaching clients my way.

OFFER TO DO A BROWN BAG LUNCH SERIES FOR THE CLIENT'S TEAM.

Set up a weekly or monthly series of educational meetings or workshops with your client's team. It is worth it to do a simple set of meetings for free, because you get to meet more potential clients and show what you can do. Or, if appropriate, ask for a small stipend for your time. This keeps you in front of your client and helps get your name out. It can also lead to coaching assignments and opportunities to train other managers and executives in the organization.

MOVE FROM COACHING TO OTHER PROFESSIONAL SERVICES.

Remember that coaching is merely one of many delivery methods to offer solutions to your clients. Be prepared to wear different hats in order to be a true trusted advisor to your clients. Look for opportunities to facilitate strategic retreats, consult, train, and—if you want—even serve as an interim executive. For instance, if you coach a client on strategy, he will almost always want to involve his executive team. This naturally leads to a set of strategic planning meetings that you can facilitate. From there, you can coach the participants to make sure that they implement the strategic priorities they have identified.

When you change from one role to another, be explicit about your role and how the scope of your work is changing. That way, you avoid any misunderstandings about your role and client expectations. If you change roles, you also have to be very careful to maintain any confidentiality agreements you have created with your coaching clients. Otherwise, you burn bridges and destroy your credibility as a professional. Aside from the ethical implications of maintaining confidentiality, the practical reality is that we live in a small world. Don't let a short-term opportunity put your long-term reputation at risk.

DO A RELATIONSHIP PLAN FOR EACH AND EVERY CLIENT.

The largest professional services firms in the world do relationship plans for their clients. That way, they anticipate opportunities where they can help, and also think about ways to build relationships throughout the organization. You should do the same, whether your client is a corporate client or an individual who has hired you for personal issues.

There are nine steps to creating a relationship plan for any given client:

Step One: Understand the business.

For a client within an organization, start by understanding the client's business. Get clear on the basics about the size of the business, its market, customers, number of employees, key financial numbers, locations, and marketing. What drives success in the client's business and industry?

Step Two: Identify and rank the client's priorities.

Before you think about what you want to sell the client, start with his top priorities. What are the current threats and opportunities that he faces? What are his biggest challenges? What are his competitors doing? What are his top strategic priorities? Focus especially on what the client has told you. It is easier to work with a client's existing priorities than it is to push what you think he should be doing onto him. Go with existing momentum!

Step Three: Come up with ways to help.

Once you know the client's top priorities, find ways that your expertise can help him to succeed. For each potential opportunity, develop a statement of your value and why the client should involve you.

Step Four: Set goals.

If you did the first three steps thoroughly, you should have a list of ways to help your current client. Now set some goals about which opportunities you will introduce by when, and how much you think each opportunity is worth to the client. How much in additional revenues can you generate from each opportunity?

Step Five: Assess the relationship with your client and improve it.

Now the relationship plan shifts from opportunities to the relationship itself, starting with your current client. What is working? How can you make the relationship better? Come up with ways to really help your client be more successful, as well as ways to better connect with him as a trusted advisor.

Step Six: Learn about other people the client knows and how you can help them.

If your client is in an organization, get the organizational chart and start learning about the other people there. Which of your client's colleagues have issues that you can help resolve? What are the other divisions in the company that could use your expertise? Assuming you have a good relationship with your client, ask him to sit down with you and give you advice about others you should know. For each person, learn as much as you can about his leadership style, opportunities, challenges, and overall aspirations.

Step Seven: Figure out how to get in front of each of these people.

Once you know whom you can help, develop a strategy to get an introduction. Will your client introduce you? Who else do you know in the organization who will make the introduction? How will you show the new prospect that you can add value?

Step Eight: Develop an overall plan.

Turn the above steps into a coherent action plan. What are the things that you will do to build relationships and introduce new opportunities? What are the things that you don't know, but need to find out? Put these in writing. That way, you have a plan you can revisit and refine over time.

Step Nine: Set a date to revisit the plan.

Within a few months, you will know more people in the client's organization. Also, the organization will face new challenges and opportunities. Therefore, revisit the plan to update it. If you have done things right, you will see even more opportunities to bring value to your original client, and everyone you have met since.

Start thinking in terms of having a 'share of mind' with each and every client. Cola companies measure their success by 'share of stomach'; that's why they've shifted from selling only soda to selling water, sports drinks, juice, and even snack foods. For coaches, the relevant metric is share of mind. You want to be top of mind for each client when he has a big challenge, so that he calls you first—regardless of whether the solution involves training, coaching, consulting, or facilitation. Similarly, you want the client's organization or network to start thinking of you first, too. What is your share of mind when a client faces his most pressing issues? Does he only think of you for coaching, and only for specific issues? Does he think of you at the same time that he thinks of other coaches and advisors? If so, you need to increase your share of mind.

The big consulting firms are great at competing for share of mind. One major technology consulting firm is famous for walking the halls and stopping in to say hello to various executives and managers. They take the credo "out of sight, out of mind" very seriously and try to never be out of sight for too long. You should start thinking that way, too. Even if you can't walk the halls every day, think about other ways to stay in touch.

Step V

BUILD A FIRM TO ENJOY LASTING WEALTH

To create a breakthrough coaching firm, you need to think like a firm builder, not a solo coach. Once you do that, you stop trading your time with clients for dollars and instead focus on building a company that is worth something and can generate an income for you while you do other things. This process starts when you develop proprietary methodologies and valuable intellectual property. Once you do, you can turn it into a portfolio of programs and products that you can offer to the market. Examples include books, information products, and tools to help your clients assess and improve their situation, certifications, and licensing arrangements. You can also contract with other coaches and experts to create larger teams that get bigger engagements so that others do part or all of the work while you make more money. Meanwhile, all of this work sets you apart even more as the go-to coaching professional in your market, attracts more clients, and allows you to charge even more money for your time.

Chapter Twenty-Three

THE FIRM-BUILDER MINDSET

By following the guidance you have read so far, you can fill your practice with high-paying, desirable clients. If you happen to coach wealthy individuals or executives in the upper echelons, you can even build your million-dollar coaching practice based on coaching clients alone. If you don't, you can attract enough clients to earn a lucrative income as a solo coach. This is a terrific position to be in because you get to enjoy a lucrative, fulfilling, and flexible career doing something you love.

However, you are leaving money on the table. There are two reasons why. First, at a certain point, every solo coach hits a ceiling in how much income he can earn. That's because every coach starts out by trading time for dollars. Even if you charge high rates, even if you charge based on value and not based on an hourly rate, even if you make more money per hour by offering group coaching and leading seminars, there is only so much time in the day. You can only take care of a limited number of clients. What if there was a way to make money even while you weren't working directly with clients?

Second, if you are a solo coach and only serve clients with custom coaching solutions, you aren't building a firm you can sell. Your business is completely dependent on you. If you go, your clients go, too. There is nothing for anyone to buy. Therefore, other than what you save from your income as a coach, you aren't creating long-term wealth. Wouldn't it be better if you were creating assets that had lots of value, even without your ongoing involvement in the business?

The way to solve both of these problems is by thinking like a firm builder instead of a solo coach. A firm builder creates leverage in his business so that he makes money even when he's not working with clients. He also creates assets, so that he builds a firm that is worth something, and that he can sell when he wants to retire or move on to other things. In other words, instead of thinking about trading time for dollars, he is thinking about building wealth.

There are two ways to get leverage and build a firm: products and other people.

Products are specific solutions that the coach creates and sells so that he makes more money in less time—including while he is sleeping, playing tennis, or spending time with family. Products include: books, subscriptions, information products, assessments, benchmarking services, and certification programs.

All coaches have the opportunity to come up with their own portfolio of products. Ideally, you come up with products for every price point in your market. That way, as many people as possible in your market can get to know you. The graphic below demonstrates this idea. At the bottom of the pyramid, you have programs that don't cost a lot, and that many people can afford. At the top, you have expensive programs that few people can afford, but that compensate you handsomely. As you go higher and higher up the pyramid, you are giving people more access to you, and charging accordingly.

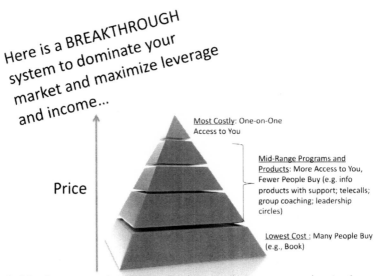

Here is a BREAKTHROUGH system to dominate your market and maximize leverage and income...

Price

Most Costly: One-on-One Access to You

Mid-Range Programs and Products: More Access to You, Fewer People Buy (e.g. info products with support; telecalls; group coaching; leadership circles)

Lowest Cost : Many People Buy (e.g., Book)

Goal: Reach as many people in your target market as possible via programs and services for clients at every price point. Maximize leverage and passive income.

Do you see the power of this model? The benefits to you are extraordinary. First, you maximize the revenue you capture from the market. Instead of offering one-on-one coaching to a select group of clients, you reach almost everyone with different programs at different price points. You increase your revenue potential exponentially. Second, you give people new ways to test you out, see the value you provide, confirm that you are credible, and then upgrade to more expensive programs. Third, you become more valuable in the process, and people are willing to pay you more money for direct, one-on-one access to you. If they aren't willing to pay for access to you, that's fine; they can pay less money and still benefit from your expertise through one or more of your other programs. Essentially, this approach allows you to escape the pay-for-time trap, so that you can make more money and gain more flexibility with your time.

Tony Robbins is a classic example of someone who built a successful product portfolio. You can benefit from Tony's wisdom by buying a book for a few dollars. Then you can pay a bit more money for an information product, which includes DVDs and additional resources besides just a book. Inside this information product, you get coupons to register at a discount for one of his weekend seminars in a packed auditorium. From there, if you can afford it, you can pay even more and join him on a group retreat on his private island. Next, you can get certified as one of his official trainers or, if you want some one-on-one time, you can pay him hundreds of thousands of dollars for private coaching. Finally, if you have a million dollars or more, you can get Tony's private phone number and call him any time. By creating all sorts of ways to gain access to his expertise, Tony has essentially created gatekeepers that make his time a rare and valuable commodity.

It doesn't matter that most of us don't have Tony Robbins' charisma or market presence. Tony simply serves as one great example of how to build a product portfolio to give and, in return, receive as much value as possible from a target market. Every coach should be thinking this way.

The second way to build a firm is through other people. There are many ways to build leverage through others:

- Contract with complementary coaches, consultants, trainers, and experts to serve your clients' needs as they arise—while you take a cut.

- License your content to others, and take a royalty or fee each time your licensees make a sale.

- Clone yourself by training other coaches who can do what you do and then either hiring them or calling them in as contractors when you have more work than you can handle or want.

Upcoming chapters in this part of the book go into more detail about some of the best options for you to build a firm through products and people. Before heading there, it is important that you understand the basic underpinning of any of these options: developing intellectual capital in the form of repeatable methodologies. The next chapter explains how to do this.

Case Study: Diversifying Your Revenue Streams
By Wendy S. Enelow, CCM, MRW, JCTC, CPRW

Wendy S. Enelow is the Founder & Executive Director of Career Thought Leaders at www.careerthoughtleaders.com, and Co-Founder & Executive Director of Resume Writing Academy at www.resumewritingacademy.com. She shares in her own words her approach to gaining market leverage with products, training programs and conferences:

One of the things I learned early on as an entrepreneur (executive resume writer and career coach) was that there were only so many billable hours each day and that I would have to find additional ways to generate revenue to meet my financial goals. Now, 32 years later, I realize how very important that insight was!

I began diversifying and opening new revenue streams with books (and now e-books), as the only investment was my time. I'm a writer by nature, so creating books was relatively easy. I then added training, which, over the years, has included in-person training and workshops, teleseminars, webcasts and other online programs. These are great since (1) people pay to attend them while you're teaching them, and (2) people pay to listen to the recorded versions and get the materials AFTER you've taught them. The latter is a great example of passive income ... earning money while you sleep ... and that is a wonderful thing!

Taking the online programs one step further, I then consolidated several onto a CD and began to sell the CDs so people could buy multiple programs at a volume discount. This has now turned into its own self-sustaining revenue stream.

Perhaps most unusual for many in the career industry, but definitely well aligned with my personal brand of building community and collaboration among career professionals, I have also hosted a number of professional career conferences. Since I founded the Career Thought Leaders Consortium, this has now become an important revenue stream. However, it must be noted that conferences are a huge commitment and a great deal of work. As I write this in July, I have spent the entire day talking to prospective speakers and writing preliminary marketing content for an event that will be happening next March! The two conferences that I currently offer each year are: Career Thought Leaders Conference

& Symposium, held in March each year; and Career Thought Leaders Global Career Brainstorming Day, held in October each year.

Running conferences can be very profitable. However, they also can pose a significant financial risk, as I'm legally contracted with our selected hotel to deliver a hefty sum of money for sleeping rooms and meals. In a nutshell, I charge people to attend the conference, pay the hotel a lot of money for meals, rooms, web access, and audiovisual equipment ... the list goes on and on. My final entrepreneurial goal: To have enough money left over to compensate me well for all of my time and effort to fill that revenue stream!

Case Study on Building a Firm and Gaining Leverage
Bill Lang International and Scores on the Board

Bill Lang has had great success as an entrepreneur, consultant, coach, author, and firm builder. He shares in his own words the way that he has built a firm that generates income for him, as well as income for licensees. More information about Bill and his company is available at www.scoresontheboard.com.

I entered the world of executive coaching after a career as a management consultant, marketing manager and Internet technology entrepreneur. After a couple of years of working with executives and managers in a number of industries, I identified a common process that worked for helping these leaders improve their performance at motivating their team members and creating self-managing teams.

I also saw an issue many of the independent coaches and consultants faced around getting leverage from their expertise and relationships. Many coaches and consultants used simple tools for assessment when working with their clients, yet found the pricing they needed to work alongside client managers was prohibitive for where the large volume of managers are – working in the front-line and middle management.

I addressed both of these problems with Scores on the Board. Scores on the Board is a coaching methodology priced to facilitate "low-human" touch coaching to the millions of team leaders and middle managers who need help but cannot afford "high-touch" 1-on-1 coaching.

I designed and tested Scores on the Board with about 50 managers and their teams. After five cycles of refinement, the five elements of the methodology and process interactions among team leaders, team members and team customers were digitized onto a cloud-based Internet platform. This included monthly feedback and improvement idea reports, 24/7 online mentoring, and process support for the team leaders and members.

Since 2006, over 3,000 team leaders, 35,000 team members and 10 million team customers have used the system. The client organizations operate in over 50 countries. Similar to the accreditation of Kaizen – Lean Sigma Black Belts, client organizations can have their staff licensed as Scores on the Board Coaches. Additionally, independent coaches and consultants are licensed to use the system with their clients.

With this program, revenues are generated from licensing of coaches, client implementation workshops and annual system license fees. The licensed coaches also earn a distribution fee from each team each year that pays the system license fee. This generates non-time based fees for coaches and consultants, freeing them up from repetitive, low-value added activity. Scores on the Board has now been published as a book written in the form of a skill and team-building fable.

Chapter Twenty-Four

HOW TO DEVELOP A FRAMEWORK
THAT TURNS INTO ONGOING WEALTH

What does Walt Disney have to do with helping coaches be successful? He took a simple piece of intellectual property, a cartoon mouse, and turned it into an empire. Mickey Mouse became the foundation of one of the most recognized brands in history, complete with movies, animation, theme parks, resorts, cruise ships, vacation clubs, a television network, and a product-licensing behemoth. In your case, you can take a single coaching framework and turn it into all sorts of products, coaching programs, seminars, training programs, licensing opportunities, and methodologies to get results for clients.

A good framework explains how to solve a pressing problem that the people in your target market have. Study any of the best-selling business and self-help authors, most of who are coaches and/or consultants, and you will see different types of frameworks:

A LIST.

Patrick Lencioni is famous for creating frameworks in list form, for instance, his books *The Five Temptations of the CEO*, *The Three Signs of a Miserable Job*, and *The Five Dysfunctions of a Team*. Stephen Covey did the same thing with his classic *The Seven Habits of Highly Successful People*. You can do the same thing. Come up with your own list of ways to identify or solve a problem. You can develop a list of steps, behaviors, attitudes, habits, challenges, requirements, competencies, forces, or drivers. Then describe what this list identifies or helps people do, be, or have.

A METHODOLOGY NAMED AFTER THE CREATOR.

The Feldenkrais Method of Somatic Education is an example of a framework using the developer's own name. Why not create a methodology named after you?

A CATCHY ACRONYM.

Neil Rackham's book *S.P.I.N. Selling* is based on the SPIN acronym for a successful selling process. My own Institute for Business Growth teaches business coaches how to help businesses be more successful with the CASTLE Model for Business Growth. My colleague Reggie Crane of Next Level Coaching and Consulting developed an acronym based on his own last name; each letter represents a way that the people in his target market, leaders in government, can improve performance. Come up with a word that captures the essence of the solution or benefit you want to bring to your clients, and turn it into an acronym.

A FOUR-SQUARE GRID.

Myers-Briggs and DiSC are well-known assessment tools many coaches use. Both are based on a four-square framework that slices up people's traits in a specific way. Similarly, the famous Situational Leadership model is a four-square grid about how to manage people based on their skill and will. If you can isolate two dimensions that define a situation or problem, the four-square grid might be a great fit for your framework development.

A METAPHOR.

David Sandler created a best-selling sales training book and a successful franchise based on his famous Sandler Sales Submarine. Each compartment of the submarine represents a different step in his selling process. There are an unlimited number of animals, minerals, vegetables, natural phenomena, and inanimate objects that can represent different types of people and problems. Other examples include: the four elements, parts of the body, emotions, geographic features, architectural styles, famous people, cultures, painting periods, car models, and so on.

A RHYME.

Bruce Tuckman's famous team development model is a great example of a rhyming framework. Even as more current models for developing successful teams come and go, nobody can forget his four stages: forming, storming, norming, and performing.

A good framework has the following characteristics:

- *Relevant.* The people in your target market find it relevant to their specific needs. Put another way, it is not generic; nobody needs yet another list of plain-vanilla leadership competencies.

- *Valuable.* It is valuable, because it helps people see their problems and opportunities in new ways that make things better for them.

- *A-ha!* It has an "a-ha!" factor, so that when people first see it, a light suddenly goes on and their thinking changes.

- *Elegant.* An elegant framework follows the rule of MECE, which is a consulting buzzword that stands for Mutually Exclusive and Collectively Exhaustive. Mutually Exclusive means that one category in your framework doesn't overlap with any other category. For instance, profit breaks down into revenues and expenses; revenues can't be expenses, and expenses can't be revenues. Collectively Exhaustive means that you have included every single possible category. In the case of profits, only revenue and expenses drive profits; there are no other categories. Creating an elegant framework is like carving a sculpture. You have to remove all of the extraneous details so that you are left with a thing of beauty.

- *Memorable.* You communicate it in a powerful, memorable way. For instance, a framework that is a list of 23 things isn't easy for anyone to remember. People have a hard time remembering more than three to five things at a time. Try to keep your framework limited to no more than five components. Similarly, use words that people can remember. What if Bruce Tuckman's four stages of a team were: starting, fighting for status and turf, contracting about proper behavior, and getting results? No one would remember them. Likewise, come up with a unique graphic to make your framework visually compelling so that it stands out.

There are a few practical ways to come up with a framework. First, write the table of contents for a book based on the framework. Some people are intimidated at the prospect of creating a framework, but everyone can write the table of contents of a book. That's pretty much the same thing! In one of my Center for Executive Coaching classes, members do an improvisational exercise in which we write the table of contents of a book in under a minute. Someone calls out a random topic for a book, like "Five Keys to Success as an Aerospace Executive." Then we brainstorm ideas for book chapters. Before we know it, we have a framework AND the table of contents for our first book as a successful expert on that topic.

A second approach is to get out a pad of Post-It Notes and start brainstorming. Write down each potential category in your framework on a single Post-It Note. Then put the notes up on a wall and start arranging and rearranging them. You might find that some ideas are subcategories of a bigger idea or grouping. Others are redundant. Keep playing around with the Post-It Notes until you have something that works.

Third, choose a graphic representation that you like, such as a four-square grid, triangle, diamond, logic tree, process flow chart—or whatever—and build your framework around it. For an example of a four-square grid, search online to see Steven Covey's time management framework, the one that has urgency on one axis and importance on the other. The Boston Consulting Group's Cash Cow model is another great example of the four-square grid. Patrick Lencioni's *Five Dysfunctions of a Team* model offers a fine example of a triangle-shaped framework. See Michael Porter's Five Competitive Forces model for an example of a framework designed in a diamond shape. The DuPont Model for Return on Investment is an example of a framework set up like a logic tree. You can get quite creative with this exercise. At the workshops that I run to help coaches develop their own unique frameworks, participants come up with all sorts of wonderful graphics, including a 3-dimensional diamond, an oak tree, a tornado, an airplane, and a house. As long as your graphic is simple, memorable, and has impact, it will work.

Fourth, get someone to interview you, and record the conversation. Your colleague should ask you all sorts of questions, as if they were cloning you so they could match your expertise. Have them ask you about the problem, the causes of the problem, and the solutions. Then make sure they drill down and ask for more details about each cause and solution. This approach works well if you are more verbally inclined. You can take the recording and hire a transcriptionist to type it out. You can edit it from there.

Fifth, get out a piece of paper and draw a mind map that represents how you think about the issue. Draw lines that connect similar ideas. Keep working on the map until you have something that is robust and comprehensive.

Sometimes a good framework comes to you quickly, and other times the process is excruciating. Be patient. Balance something that is sloppy and superficial with the drive to create something perfect. Be willing to develop something that seems good enough, test it with trusted colleagues, and then revise it based on feedback.

Once you have even a single framework, you are on the verge of building a successful, valuable firm. You set yourself apart as a credible expert with a powerful solution. You have the foundation to create products that will earn you money while you do other things. You can train other people—whether through certifications, licensing, or your internal development program—so that they can apply your framework while you make money. Best of all, you have an asset that generates wealth for you over the long haul.

Start now…. choose a problem that you know your target market faces. Come up with a rough draft framework that identifies the main causes of the problem and how people can solve it.

Case Study: The Power of Having a Framework
By Melissa Pahl, Owner, Twenty Marketing, www.TwentyMarketing.com

One of the biggest challenges a coach or consultant faces is boiling down their years of experience and expertise into manageable, bite-sized chunks for their clients. Creating a framework that is uniquely yours is one of the most powerful ways to solve this dilemma.

Creating a framework puts you in the driver's seat versus just reacting to your clients. It also reduces overwhelm for your client—they see that you have a plan in place before you even get started. But one of the greatest benefits you will receive by creating your own framework is that it will differentiate you from your competition.

Here's a quick example. I provide marketing coaching and consulting, and my clients often come to me saying they need to do something with their website. My overall marketing approach is to start with my client's customers and back the marketing up to match what their customers need. Depending on the product, often a website really doesn't do that much for a company. But it's never a good idea to tell a client they are wrong!

In this case, I have a sub-framework that I rely heavily on that starts with, and then expands from, three simple questions: First, what questions do you want your website to answer? Second, how does your website fit into your sales cycle? Third, how do your customers use your website now? The client's answers lead me to deeper questions, based on my framework.

In addition to the benefits noted above, having a framework like this one brings two additional benefits to me. Number one, clients relax because they feel as if they are dealing with an expert, not just someone trying to make a sale. Number two, my framework allows me to pull a client back from a solution I don't think will give them good results. Then, I am in a better position to do what I'm best at—designing effective marketing based on the end consumer.

I highly encourage you to create frameworks within your business.

Chapter Twenty-Five

TWELVE STEPS TO A SUCCESSFUL BOOK

A book can generate additional income for you, and it can also bring many valuable benefits to your practice. Having a book is a powerful marketing tool—much more effective than any glossy brochure you could print. It shows that you are an expert. It gives you instant credibility. It helps you to deepen your intellectual capital and crystallize it in writing.

Clearly, the upside of writing a book is high. At the same time, the downside risk is low. In today's age of digital, on-demand printing, you don't have to spend much money to produce or print a book. When I self-published my first book, it was before on-demand printers existed. I had to order 1,500 copies from my printer. Then I had to store all of those books in a self-storage facility. Today you can order a single copy of your book, so your printing and storage costs are negligible.

Following are twelve steps to get your book out to your target market. You can adapt this process to create eBooks, CDs, DVDs, business school-style case studies, games, and training simulations—all of which also bring you additional revenues and add to your credibility. However, there is something magical about having a printed book, especially one that is professionally designed and produced. It simply gives you more credibility than other products do.

ONE: GET YOUR PRIORITIES STRAIGHT.

Approximately 850,000 new books become available every year, and there are three million books available to you online and in bookstores right now. Very few of these are going to become best sellers or make more than hot dog money for the authors. While it would be great to see your name on one of the *New York Times* bestseller lists, it is unlikely.

You are a coach first, and an author second. You can make money marketing your book. However, if you try to market your book so that you become a best-selling author while running a coaching practice, you will spread yourself too thin. For instance, I know an author who tries to make his living selling nothing but his books. Every week he travels to a new bookstore or other venue to speak about his book, sign copies, stay overnight in a motel, and travel to the next venue in the morning. He makes a fair living that way, but it's not a living most of us want, and it's a very different business model than being a coach.

Use your book to help you demonstrate that you are credible, build your coaching practice, and open up new opportunities for you—while also selling it as a source of income where it makes sense. For instance, my first book was *Elegant Leadership: Simple Strategies, Remarkable Results*. The book is a field guide about how to become a more effective leader. It contains hundreds of worksheets that readers can fill in to become better in just about every aspect of leadership. I leave it with my prospects to give them examples of the types of coaching and training programs I can do for them. By sharing my approach to leadership development with concrete examples, many of these prospects hire me. It also gets me speaking engagements and offers from all sorts of business partners interested in licensing my content. I have sold only about 5,000 copies of this book, but made well into the millions through the client engagements and business partnerships that this book has made possible for me. I never could have made this much money if I didn't have my priorities straight: coaching first, and book sales second.

TWO: COME UP WITH A PLAN FOR WHAT YOU WANT YOUR READERS TO DO WHEN THEY FINISH YOUR BOOK.

If your top priority is for your book to build your credibility and attract clients, then make sure that your book has an upsell in the back. Make an offer that gives the reader a chance to learn more about you. For instance, give people a coupon code to go to your website and purchase an information product at a discount. Tell readers how to contact you for a free coaching assessment. Give a password to an exclusive member area where you include some podcasts and videos, and continue to build your relationship with them—while collecting their contact information so you can send them your newsletter. Thanks to digital printing, it is easy to test different offers and then change them around when you print the next batch of books.

THREE: REALIZE THAT YOU DON'T NEED A TRADITIONAL PUBLISHER.

Traditional publishers are not set up to serve the needs of most coaches. First, they are too slow. To get to a publisher, you first need to get an agent, and that can take months. Then the agent needs to find and negotiate with a publisher, and that can take many more months. Then the publisher needs to get its act together to get the book on the market, and that can take a year from when you finish the book. After all of that, you still need to promote your book as if you had published it on your own, because publishers no longer do much for new authors in that regard.

Remember your top priority—to get a book out in order to build credibility and attract clients. If you are the type who feels tempted by the idea of a traditional publisher, perhaps out of vanity or the desire to make your parents proud, think twice! You can do everything on your own that traditional publishers do—except faster. You can hire editors and designers on sites like elance.com. You can print your book through digital services like lulu.com. You can purchase an ISBN, or book bar code, so that your book is available on online bookstores. You can also purchase a distribution arrangement through your digital printer, so that you reach brick-and-mortar bookstores through a major distributor like Ingram—or you can reach out to distributors on your own.

One option worth exploring is the hybrid publisher. A hybrid publisher designs and distributes your book much more quickly than a traditional publisher, while giving you a menu of à la carte services to promote your book. For instance, the publisher of this book, Morgan James, uses this model. This is my third book with them, and I have been very pleased with the results.

Remember that the bulk of the work in book writing is in promoting your book. Whether you have a traditional publisher, a hybrid publisher, or you do it yourself, you are still responsible for the bulk of that work. Given this reality, be very careful about choosing to go the traditional publishing route.

FOUR: DEVELOP YOUR CATCHY TITLE AND SUBTITLE.

Before you write your book, come up with a catchy title and subtitle. Make sure that your title has clear appeal to your target market. It must compel them to want to read your book, and make a clear promise of the benefits and value readers will get from the book. Your title should speak to the people in your target market by using language that they speak. Check out the list of current and past best-selling book titles, and model your title on what these authors have done. Jay Conrad Levinson's original Guerrilla Marketing book is a great example of a title and subtitle to emulate—*Guerrilla Marketing: Easy and Inexpensive Strategies for Making Big Profits from Your Small Business.* He captures the reader's attention with the guerrilla metaphor. His title clearly focuses on the issue of marketing, while his subtitle clearly targets small business owners. It also promises that the book provides marketing strategies with three benefits: easy, inexpensive, and big profits.

FIVE: DESIGN A COVER THAT LOOKS LIKE A BOOK FROM A TRADITIONAL PUBLISHER.

Go to your local bookstore and see which business books catch your eye first and make the author seem especially credible. Find a few covers that you really like, and figure out what the designer has done to grab your attention. What colors stand out most? What fonts? What images? What kinds of blurbs? Then hire a book designer to mock up some covers for you. Like it or not, people do judge a book by its cover. You don't want a book that looks as though it was self-published. Invest some money in a strong, memorable, professional-looking cover.

SIX: DEVELOP A TIGHT TABLE OF CONTENTS.

Your table of contents should reflect your framework for solving a pressing problem. A good table of contents shows readers that you have a unique, valuable point of view about the world. It also makes it easier for you to organize your thoughts and write the book.

SEVEN: FIND THE MOST EFFICIENT PATH TO WRITE THE BOOK.

Writing a book does not have to be as intimidating as many people think it is. First, more and more people want to read short books and short chapters; this growing market preference makes it much easier for authors to write.

Second, it doesn't take that long to write a book if you are disciplined about it. If you can write three pages a day, you can have a 150-page book in about two months. If you write a newsletter every week, you can make each issue a chapter of your book, and have a book in less than a year. If you prefer to speak, sit down with a microphone and give a series of impromptu lectures about each topic in your table of contents. You can hire someone to transcribe your lectures on elance.com.

Third, you don't have to do all of the writing. Get others to contribute chapters, while you remain the primary editor and author. Marshall Goldsmith did this with Laurence S. Lyons for his book about coaching, *Coaching for Leadership: The Practice of Leadership Coaching from the World's Greatest Coaches*.

You can also interview one expert for each chapter of the book. Record the interview, transcribe it, and use it as a complete chapter. My friend Corey Crowder and I did that for our book *Success in a Challenging World*. We interviewed 24 successful African Americans and dedicated a chapter to each. All we had to do was edit the interviews and write an introduction and conclusion.

Worst case, you can go to elance.com and hire a ghostwriter to interview you and write the book based on what you have to say.

EIGHT: EDIT THE BOOK.

It is essential to hire a professional editor to get rid of typos and grammatical errors and strengthen your writing where needed. A Google search will get you a list of editing services, or you can find freelance editors on elance.com.

NINE: DESIGN THE BOOK'S INTERIOR.

Digital printers and eBook vendors have formatting requirements that must be met for them to print or distribute your book. These requirements are not very complicated, and some of you can figure them out on your own. Unfortunately,

I was not born with that ability, and I'm too lazy to develop it now. So I hire a graphic designer to design the interior of each book along with the cover.

TEN: PRINT THE BOOK.

There are a growing number of on-demand printers that can print as little as one copy. I use lulu.com and, without receiving any compensation in return, recommend them. You can do a Google search to find many others and compare prices and services. Many of these on-demand printers offer publishing packages as well.

ELEVEN: MARKET THE BOOK IN WAYS THAT DON'T DISTRACT FROM MARKETING YOUR COACHING PRACTICE.

For more information on marketing your book, get *Guerrilla Marketing for Writers* by Jay Conrad Levinson, Rick Frishman, and Michael Larsen. In my own experience, the best ways to market your book, while also setting yourself up to attract clients and get coaching engagements, include:

- Feature your book prominently on your website.

- Let the people on your list know about your book.

- Ask the people in your network to send out emails telling others to buy the book.

- Offer free webinars and telecalls about different topics in your book. Promote these to your list, as well as to associations. For instance, to promote the book *Guerrilla Marketing for a Bulletproof Career,* I did a number of webinars for university career offices and career associations.

- Use the book as a vehicle to get booked as a speaker, and offer it for sale at the back of the room.

- Use your social media presence to market the book. In addition to the major social media sites, set up your author profile on filedby.com, a social media site for authors.

- Mention the book in your blogs and articles.

- Ask high-profile bloggers in your market to let you write a guest blog based on information in the book.

- Issue press releases in your local media about the book.

- Reach out to media and offer yourself as an expert; use the book to prove your credibility. The key to success is promoting your expertise about topical issues, not promoting your book. If you have the budget, consider hiring a seasoned publicist to market you as an expert and get you media visibility. This is an expensive investment and won't directly sell books or get you clients. However, if you get interviewed, you can promote yourself as someone who has been seen or heard on major media outlets and shows.

- Market your book in large quantities to relevant institutions and associations to buy for their employees or members. Many corporations buy books en masse for their employees. Similarly, you can offer your book to vendors for them to give to their customers as a premium. For instance, if you market a book for physicians, you might find a drug company that buys it as a premium to give to medical practices.

TWELVE: KEEP YOUR EYE ON YOUR PRIORITIES, AND WATCH OUT FOR THE TEMPTATION OF VANITY.

Once you have a book, you will face many temptations to spend your money, and time, to market the book. These investments can detract from your coaching practice, and actually end up hurting your income. In my own case, I am constantly bombarded with offers to spend anywhere from $8,500 up to $50,000 for publicity campaigns, speaker booking services, and paid advertising for my books. I am fortunate that, when I get these offers, my wife quickly reminds me of our family's priorities. I am not in this game to be famous. I do care about paying for our children's college education and securing our future—while doing work that I love. Therefore, my goal with each and every book that I write remains the same: attract great clients, get great results, and build a profitable firm. Books are one of many vehicles to get me there.

Chapter Twenty-Six

INFORMATION PRODUCTS TO GET UP TO 100 TIMES THE PRICE OF A BOOK

What if, instead of getting $20 up to $99 for your book, you could get hundreds or even thousands of dollars for an information product that includes pretty much the same content as your book? An information product is a package of information that gives the people in your target market step-by-step guidance to solve a pressing problem or seize a compelling opportunity on their own. Depending on your product, an information product can be as simple as an eBook that people download, along with some email support. From there, you can add to the features by including one or more printed books, audio CDs, DVDs with video, a member area filled with resources, live telecalls with you, software, templates of key documents like legal contracts or marketing materials, premium newsletter subscription or trial, and a personal orientation call.

There is a market for information products because many people face complex issues, and they want simple answers. When they search for solutions on the Internet, they are overwhelmed by too much data from too many questionable sources. They feel as if they only get bits and pieces of information from each source, and many experts contradicts one another. That's why people need someone like you to simplify all of the random facts and sources of information out there, and turn it into a step-by-step, paint-by-number system that they can use to get results. The key to developing a successful information product is to give people a system that gives them a complete and comprehensive way to solve a problem on their own.

At the same time, many people want a lower-cost alternative to a full coaching engagement. Some of them would love to hire you, but don't have the money for a full-blown coaching engagement; they can still afford to pay you handsomely for your information, if you package it properly and at a price that fits their budget. Others have the money to hire you as a coach, but need to try a solution on their own before hiring you for more guidance. Either way, both of you win.

Information products are also wonderful for another reason. Over time, you might find that you make more money marketing information products than coaching. Eventually you hit a tipping point where you can choose whether to coach clients or not, because information products generate that much income for you. I remember when this happened for me. Suddenly I had total flexibility in the clients I chose, how much I charged, and whether to terminate engagements or keep them going. Clients sensed a change in my attitude because I was no longer dependent on them to make a good living. They had more respect for me, and this gave me the confidence to raise my fees and make even more money—while choosing to work with only the very best clients for my style and preferences. Meanwhile, I got to play tennis just about every day mid-morning. During breaks between odd games, I could check my email and see new orders for information products come through. It was as if I was getting paid to play tennis!

Here are ten steps for you to create information products of your own:

STEP ONE: IDENTIFY A COMPELLING PROBLEM OR OPPORTUNITY TO ADDRESS.

The more compelling the problem or opportunity that your market faces, the more likely you are to have buyers. Fortunately, there are almost unlimited possibilities. People in almost every target market have common problems and opportunities that they want to address, if only they had the right system: how to make more money, save time, start specific businesses, get healthier, find a mate, find the ideal job, retire securely, be better parents, have happier marriages, improve their memory, get stronger, be more persuasive, overcome limiting beliefs, be more productive, be more attractive, build a stronger network, take a business to the next level, turn a business over to children, pay less taxes, and identify new ways to get customers.

Whichever issue you choose, target it so that it appeals to your specific niche. That way, you develop a focused solution instead of offering a generic information product. As noted earlier in this book, you might have a smaller number of prospects when you focus, but your conversion rate from prospect to buyer more than makes up for this.

STEP TWO: CREATE A COMPREHENSIVE SYSTEM.

Develop the features that come with your information product. The first paragraph in this chapter gave you a list of potential features. Choose enough features to solve the buyer's whole problem. For instance, if you are creating an information product to help parents manage their overweight child's diet, your information product might include: an overview of good nutrition, a daily calorie tracker, daily recipes for six months, shopping lists, weight tracking tools, exercise routines, exercise journals, email support from a registered nutritionist, and perhaps an online member area to plan menus and track calories. Similarly, if you were creating an information product for fitness professionals to add boxing fitness to their routines, you might include a manual and set of videos with: equipment lists, gym design, safety assessment forms, how to assess the fitness client, basic stance and punches, warm-up routines, shadow-boxing routines, cool-off routines, sample workouts for groups and private lessons, marketing materials to attract clients, and information about getting proper insurance. You might also offer an option to include an equipment starter kit with wraps, mouthpieces, gloves, and focus mitts.

STEP THREE: DON'T BE A PERFECTIONIST.

You don't have to roll out a perfect product. It is better to test a product that might have some gaps, and let the buyers tell you what you need to do to improve it. Don't guess, or else you might provide more than you need to. Worse, you might be so much of a perfectionist that you'll never feel comfortable releasing anything. It is better to get something out to your market on a trial basis and observe how people react.

For instance, my Center for Executive Coaching started out as a single book and CDs with ten group telecalls. As more people joined, I added to the features. Now it includes: five manuals; an extensive member area; tons of one-on-one support; an ongoing series of telecalls; in-person workshops; sister sites for business, career coaching, and sales coaching; and approval as a provider of training hours for the International Coach Federation.

STEP FOUR: CREATE A GREAT OFFER.

In addition to the features of your program, your offer includes: pricing, installment payments, your guarantee or pledge, and free bonuses. To finalize your prices, choose three prices to test—low, high, and in the middle. Set up a period of time in which to test each, starting with the lowest price, and see which offer makes you the most money. Over time, you can always increase prices, either through additional testing or by adding new, more valuable features to your information product. While testing your price, also test whether offering installments increases how many people buy. Making the price more digestible often increases sales, but you have to balance that increase with the added delinquencies you will have to deal with.

You should also test whether guarantees increase sales or not, when compared to returns. Sometimes guarantees increase sales, and other times—no matter how good your product is—buyers act as if your site is the local library. They order your program and return it quickly, probably after making a copy for their own benefit. If a money-back guarantee won't work, come up with a pledge that combines a number of softer promises, like turnaround time for support, the quality of the content, and the fact that—if people follow your system—they will see results.

Finally, test out whether it increases sales to add a few free bonuses, even if those bonuses are things that you planned to include anyway.

STEP FIVE: WRITE GREAT COPY.

There is an art to writing effective copy for an information product. Study some of the information products that are out there, and identify which elements of the copy suck you in and get you in the mood to buy. Keep a file folder of effective headlines, opening paragraphs, sub-headings, the overall logic flow, use of testimonials, description of benefits and features, ways to position the price, and transitions from one point to another.

There are some reasonably priced copywriters whom you can find on elance.com and other freelance sites. Look for someone skilled at writing copy for information products. Check out their samples, and make sure you like their approach.

As always, test different copy and keep improving results.

STEP SIX: DEVELOP A WAY TO TAKE AND FULFILL ORDERS.

If you don't already have it, you need to have the proper infrastructure to take online orders. The key elements include a shopping cart that takes orders and a relationship with a credit card processor to process credit card orders. Your web designer might have an off-the-shelf shopping cart program that they use, or they might build one for you. I have tried both and have gotten good results from 1ShoppingCart at www.1shoppingcart.com. Authorize.net is one of the largest credit card processors, and they can set you up with the various applications you need to get started. PayPal also offers a credit card processing service. You can also check with big banks like Bank of America for their merchant services accounts. Be sure to check ongoing fees and percentage fees carefully, because there is wide variation and it is easy to get burned.

STEP SEVEN: SET UP WAYS TO TRACK VISITORS AND CONVERSION.

Online marketing is incredible; you can track almost everything that happens on your website. Work with your developer to set up robust analytics on your site. You need to know how many visitors come to different pages of your site, how long they stay, how many end up on your thank-you-for-ordering page, and how they got there. If you use tools like Google AdWords, carefully track the keywords and ad variations that work best for you, and optimize them. Every time you change your offer, copy, or anything else on your site, track results and see whether traffic and conversion gets better or worse. Track everything, all the time! It doesn't cost anything, and it will make a huge difference in how quickly you can create profits from your information programs.

STEP EIGHT: GET THE WORD OUT.

There are many similarities between marketing your book and marketing your information products. Most of the advice in the previous chapter about book marketing applies. For instance, whenever you speak, you can offer your information program at the back of the room or through an order form that you give to participants with a special deal. However, with information products, you can get more sophisticated because your margins are higher. For instance:

Test Google AdWords and other pay-per-click advertising programs. Track how much it takes to get an order, and which words are profitable. Then continue to optimize your account. As long as you can get an order for less than it takes you to fulfill it, you are making money. Sometimes pay per click works, and sometimes the words in your market are simply too expensive to make sense.

Use Search Engine Optimization, or SEO. Once you know that you have a profitable information product, it can be worth it to hire a qualified SEO expert to increase your search engine rankings. As always, make any expert accountable for results, and track results carefully to make sure your profits exceed your investment.

Launch one or more dedicated websites for your information product, in addition to offering it on your coaching website. With dedicated websites, you can test different online marketing strategies. Start with a site that has a long sales letter, including a place for people to sign up for an email newsletter or free report. Also test out a single squeeze page that features a video of you describing the product and a free report that people can sign up for. After people sign up for the free report, send them to a long sales letter that tries to convert them. Meanwhile, you can follow up with visitors to your site with an email marketing campaign to convince them to take action and buy your information product.

Set up an affiliate program. Affiliates are people who sign up to market your programs in exchange for a commission. For instance, www.shareasale.com is an affiliate management site that lets you track affiliate sales, upload banners and graphics for affiliates, and send out special offers to affiliates. I must confess that, despite trying, I haven't made much money through affiliates. I have found many scammers making false promises about the results they can get for me if I would only hire them for a large affiliate marketing consulting engagement. If you are interested in affiliate marketing, do your due diligence and be willing to invest the time in managing your affiliates, giving them the support they need to succeed, and keeping them motivated.

STEP NINE: INCLUDE AN UPSELL.

Include an offer for the next program or service for the buyer to purchase. Keep following up with buyers to convert them to that next level of access to you. Notice what is happening here. Your book readers get a coupon to purchase your information product. Your information product buyers get a coupon to purchase a seminar, membership in a leadership circle, or coaching program. Before you know it, a $20 book or a $200 information product generates tens of thousands of dollars, all from a single buyer. That's why some authors basically give their books away at cost or even for free—because they have a system in place to keep selling the next thing to buyers.

STEP TEN: BECOME A STUDENT OF THE INFORMATION MARKETING GAME.

Information marketing is an industry in and of itself. There are many, many blogs, conferences, and self-proclaimed experts in this arena. Take advantage of the free information and telecalls that these experts offer, and learn all you can. Test different approaches and discover what works for you. Study other information products offered online, and test out some of the things they are doing that seem to be selling well.

Chapter Twenty-Seven

GROUP-COACHING PACKAGES, SEMINARS, SUBSCRIPTIONS, AND LEADERSHIP CIRCLES

You can create leverage by offering services to groups. That way, you make more money in less time by providing a service to multiple clients simultaneously. There are many ways to do this. You already read about Wendy Enelow's success running conferences, in Chapter Twenty-Three. This chapter covers four additional strategies.

The first of these is a no-brainer for most coaches: group-coaching packages. If you charge $1,500 per month for a single client, why not charge $1,000 per person for a six-person group-coaching package? In this example, you make four times more money for the same amount of your time. Group coaching is a great way to work with clients who don't have the budget for one-on-one coaching, a common approach to working with a client's direct reports, and also a smart program to offer one-on-one clients who are ready for a maintenance program. Also, as you grow your practice, you can train other coaches to run some of your group-coaching sessions, while taking a nice cut of the fees.

The second is seminars. Seminars are a good fit for most coaches, because you can take your content and offer it in an intensive in-person format. At the same time, many people in your target market want answers fast and prefer to meet over a couple of days rather than months to get those answers. Seminars achieve this goal for them. Seminars can also be a powerful starting point for your coaching clients. For instance, I like my business coaching clients to go through a two-day seminar to learn about my system for business growth, assess their opportunities to improve the business, and get up to speed before the weekly coaching begins. Finally, seminars are the perfect way for prospects to test you out, see the value you can provide, and then choose to sign up for additional coaching to keep making progress.

A seminar is a great upsell for your book and information product buyers. Based on what you have read in this and the previous two chapters, you should now see one way to sequence your offers. Start with a book, which you can give away at cost, and which makes an offer for your information product. The information product contains an offer for a seminar. At the seminar, you can convert people to group and one-on-one coaching programs.

You don't have to do it this way, and every program you offer can have various upsells, but this particular sequence has been proven to work. For instance, one entrepreneur hired a marketing company to distribute roughly 50,000 books for free, plus a $6.95 shipping and handling fee. Each book offered a coupon to a $200 information product. The book, along with a carefully executed email marketing campaign, led to the sale of 2,500 such products, for a total of $500,000 in revenues. The information product offered a ticket to a $3,000 seminar. This offer, again combined with email marketing, sold 800 tickets, or $2.4 million. The $2.9 million in revenues from selling the information product and seminar more than paid for the marketing expert's fees and printing of the books—and led to some very lucrative one-on-one coaching contracts, too. Now, I don't suggest that you take the risk of hiring an expensive marketing expert and print tens of thousands of books right out of the gate. For now, get your book out there, and include upsells to additional programs, including a seminar. Once you learn the game, you can take bigger and bigger risks.

The third program that gives you leverage is subscriptions. With a subscription, you offer a monthly, quarterly, or annual fee to members in exchange for a collection of valuable services to your target market. Because you can set your shopping cart to charge each member's credit or debit card automatically, you can generate a sizeable stream of recurring revenue with subscriptions. As long as you provide ongoing value, most members won't cancel. Also, a subscription is not so different from a gym membership. Just as gym members keep paying, even when they don't visit the gym regularly, you will also find that your subscribers keep paying, even if they don't take regular advantage of all of the services you offer them.

You don't have to create a complicated subscription program. For instance, you already read about Marc Pitman, the Fundraising Coach, who offers a premium subscription to his newsletter. While he offers a free monthly newsletter, he charges a small monthly fee to people who would prefer weekly motivation and tips about raising funds.

You can add many more features to your subscriptions: weekly or monthly live telecalls, a member's area where members can get valuable content, polling of members about best practices, access to other members for networking; online classes that follow a weekly or monthly curriculum, and interviews with industry experts. In my own case, one of my subscription sites even has the capability of automatically adding more content to each member's area, based on how long they have been a member. That gives members the perception of constantly increasing value.

The fourth example of leverage through groups is a leadership circle. There are many programs on the market that bring together business leaders for a monthly meeting where they can network, share problems, hear from experts, and develop new insights to run their companies. Examples include Vistage, The Alternative Board, The Young President's Organization, and Renaissance Executive Forums. The typical monthly agenda is simple. First, after a little bit of networking, each member shares how his business is going. Next, the facilitator provides some educational content, either on his own or by inviting a speaker in. Finally, one member talks about his business in depth, while getting support and advice from other members. In between meetings, the group facilitator checks in with members, provides a set number of coaching hours and—of course—looks for opportunities to provide additional services. You can create your own group without joining a franchise, and charge members an ongoing fee for participation.

You can also run a national leadership circle, which meets less frequently but still provides valuable services to members. For instance, the founder of a healthcare advisory firm runs leadership circles that target top executives of the top hospital in each major market. His leadership circles are exclusively for CEOs. Each of these leadership circles has about 100 CEOs who pay $10,000 per year for membership. That's $1 million dollars—and he currently has two of these going. The members form a board of advisors that determine the agenda for each group. He provides them with a set of research papers of best practices on key issues they face, quick polls of members when another member is facing an issue, and a quarterly in-person conference. This program has been so successful that he is rolling out lower-cost leadership circles specifically for Chief Operating Officers, Chief Information Officers, and Chief Medical Officers.

There are many niches available for leadership circles related to specific industries, job titles, genders, ethnicities, religious affiliations, life-cycle stages, and more.

Starting one of these groups on the fly can require a backbreaking amount of prospecting before you recruit enough members to have critical mass. In fact, some franchises charge their franchisees a hefty fee to provide cold-calling services on their behalf. Before you jump into this model, call some of the above-mentioned franchises and organizations and learn as much as you can from them. Find out what it really takes to build a successful group from scratch.

For most coaches, there are two ways to build a leadership circle without resorting to cold-calling. The first is to fill your coaching practice with clients first. Then after you have proved your value to them, invite these clients to join a leadership circle. That way, you build your leadership circle based on your trusted business relationships. A second way to build your leadership circle is by finding a sponsor. For instance, a local bank might pay you to run a leadership circle for their commercial banking clients. A business broker, angel investor, and private equity investor might do the same.

Give some thought to group coaching, seminars, subscriptions, and leadership circles. All of these provide you with leverage because you serve many clients at once, and because you build on previous sales. The group-coaching alternative should be an obvious choice for most coaches. However, seminars, subscriptions, and leadership circles can also bring in excellent revenue streams.

Chapter Twenty-Eight

CERTIFY OTHERS AND/OR LICENSE YOUR CONTENT

Y ou have read that an information product gives you the ability to charge as much as 100 times more than a traditional paperback book. With a certification or licensing program, you can charge ten or more times the price of an information product. A certification sets someone apart as having unique and valuable knowledge. It is a credential that gives status and the ability to earn more money. For this reason, people are willing to pay lots of money to get certified, and you can create a lucrative income stream by certifying them.

A license takes certification one step further by granting certified individuals permission to use your content in exchange for royalties or a materials fee. That way, you receive a payment every time one of your licensees uses your proprietary intellectual property with a client.

Certifications and licensing open up a stream of new revenues for you, including: a training fee for people to get certified, a testing fee, annual recertification fees, materials fees, and royalties.

Now, you might think that certifications and licenses are extremely complicated to create. This is not true. A certification program is basically an information product that includes a testing and certification process. People can complete the program from their homes or through in-person training. You decide how rigorous the testing process will be for certification, and it can range from a multiple-choice test to practice hours, a written exam, role-plays, and an in-depth interview process. Just be sure to check with an attorney about the laws in your state with regard to offering certifications, the terms and conditions to include, and how to avoid liability. If it makes you more comfortable, offer a Certificate of Completion for completing your program rather than formal certification.

A licensing arrangement gets a bit more complicated. Before you license your content, engage an intellectual property attorney. He can give you in-depth advice and write an agreement that protects your intellectual capital and assures that you get paid by licensees. He can also help you to make sure that you are creating a licensing deal and not a franchise, which requires much more stringent and expensive legal documents and reporting. Don't ignore this advice: If you call something a license when it is really a franchise, the legal consequences could be severe.

My wife, Elena, and I have built up a stream of income from a variety of certification and train-the-trainer programs. Please see Elena's site www.etiquettemoms.com. This is a site that trains people to teach children, teens, and adults how to use proper etiquette. Participants study the materials in the comfort of their home and then submit a test when they are ready. It's that simple, and Elena now has trained trainers from 53 countries around the world. She has also developed an image-consulting certification program, now available at www.instituteforimageconsulting.com.

In my case, I offer two types of certification programs. First, I certify people to be executive coaches, business coaches, career coaches, and sales trainers/coaches. Go to www.coachtrainingcompany.com for a list of these programs and how they work. By offering these programs, I not only make additional income, I also get some other terrific benefits. First, I grow my network of coaches who can refer me to their clients and vice versa. Second, I am constantly delighted and surprised by the number of inquiries I get from around the world from people who want me to either coach them or train the people in their organizations to be coaches. Having a coach training company sets me apart as a top-tier coach. Third, I get to constantly develop my coaching skills by learning about what my members are doing. Fourth, it is incredibly gratifying to see the members of my program succeed and raise the bar of what it means to be a successful coach.

Once a coach gets certified in my programs, they have the option to get a second, more advanced certification. This certification allows them to train other individuals to become coaches. To do that, they need to go through a rigorous, highly intensive training program. They also have to agree to pay a materials and certification fee for each individual they train.

In addition to training and certifying executive-level coaches, I also provide training programs for fitness trainers. I got into this when I was working with an incredible boxing fitness trainer. I approached him with the idea of creating a boxing fitness training and certification program for other fitness trainers. From there, I've developed certification programs with other top-tier fitness professionals in the areas of kickboxing, self-defense, strength training, agility, and training elite youth athletes. See www.fitnessnichecompany.com to learn how these programs work.

By now you are probably wondering, "What exactly qualifies you, me, or anyone else to offer a certification program?" To earn the right to offer a certification program, you need credibility. Credibility comes from any or all of the following:

- Confidence in yourself as an expert.

- Proven, valuable, proprietary intellectual content to back up that confidence. This content can include tools, a framework, or a coaching methodology that has gotten great results with clients.

- A compelling story that you can tell about your expertise, results, or how you developed your system.

- Social proof through testimonials and references about your expertise and certification materials.

- More social proof through your personal or firm brand, including having a well-received book or information product, being visible in your market, and developing expert status. In other words, you have followed the advice you have read so far in these chapters.

- Affiliations with organizations that people already perceive to be valid. For instance, my executive-level coaching programs are approved by the International Coach Federation to offer training hours, and for continuing education with the Human Resources Certification Institute. My business-coaching program is approved for continuing education with NASBA, the National Association of State Boards of Accountancy. My fitness programs receive continuing education units from a variety of respected fitness associations.

- Setting up a board of advisors made up of opinion leaders in your field.

- Building up your network to include the movers and shakers in your field.

- The success of your certified students.

One can't help but think of the Wizard of Oz giving the scarecrow the gift of brains:

"Back where I come from we have universities, seats of great learning—where men go to become great thinkers. And when they come out, they think deep thoughts—and with no more brains than you have...But! They have one thing you haven't got! A diploma! Therefore, by virtue of the authority vested in me by the Universitatus Committeeatum e plurbis unum, I hereby confer upon you the honorary degree of Th.D. .... That's Dr. of Thinkology!"

On receiving his diploma, the scarecrow has instant confidence and recites Pythagoras' Theorem.

Take some time to come up with at least one idea for a certification program that you can offer people in your marketplace. Don't worry about how to get it done yet. Instead, think about a program that no one else is offering that can give people a credential that they value, and that makes a contribution to your field. Remember that you can certify both clients and coaches in your methodology.

Once you have an idea, answer these questions:

- What is the value proposition of your certification? Why should people pay you to get certified?
- What is the minimum product you can roll out and test, given that you can expand your offering over time based on participant feedback?
- What materials will you provide?
- How will you train participants?
- Will you offer self-paced learning, a schedule of webinars or teleclasses, and/or in-person classroom training?
- What does it take to get certified in your program?
- What ongoing support will you offer?
- How much will you charge at first, given that you can always raise prices as you go?
- Based on the list provided above, how will you prove your credibility to be offering a certification?

- Where can you apply to offer continuing education units or get approved by a leading association?

- What, if anything, will you charge for annual renewals, testing, a licensing fee, or materials?

- What kinds of advanced certification can you offer after people achieve a first level of certification?

- How can you license your content in ways that generate materials or other fees for use by people you have certified?

What About Starting a Franchise?

If you develop a successful coaching or professional services firm, including a step-by-step system for success, creating a franchise might be an option for you. Dozens of coaching and business advisory franchises have sprung up over the past years. Some have made their founders very wealthy. There is no reason why you can't start your own franchise. However, starting a franchise involves significant, expensive legal and reporting requirements. It also takes a lot of work and capital to recruit new franchisees, train them, and keep them happy. Along with the fact that they aren't selling cheese pizza but rather a highly personalized, hard-to-replicate service, many business services franchises struggle with high turnover among both employees and franchisees. The market for business services franchises is no longer wide open, as it was a couple of decades ago.

If starting a franchise is an option you wish to explore, do lots of due diligence before you jump in. For instance, check out the franchises in the coaching, consulting, and business advisory space. Contact a couple of franchise consultants and get their opinions. Ask for a consultation with a franchise attorney so that you know how much it will cost to assemble the many legal documents required, and what it costs to recruit a franchisee.

Otherwise, stick with the much simpler, but still potentially lucrative, certification and/or licensing options.

Chapter Twenty-Nine

GET BIGGER ENGAGEMENTS BY CONTRACTING WITH OR HIRING OTHER COACHES AND EXPERTS

I f you can get clients, you are in a great position, because many coaches can't. They are neither comfortable with nor good at developing new business—even if they are great coaches. Many coaches are hungry and will take work at lower-than-normal fees if they don't have to generate the lead or close the deal. Meanwhile, the person who controls the client controls the terms of the deal. That's you! This gives you the opportunity to hire in other coaches and earn a profit from their work in addition to your own.

The Internet makes it easier than ever to create a virtual firm. Through LinkedIn, you can develop a network of coaches, consultants, and other experts who you can call into client engagements when appropriate. You can also form alliances with your colleagues, based on complementary skills, and go after bigger clients than you could ever get alone.

A virtual firm lets you scale up and down with each engagement by hiring contractors. You don't have to have employees who you have to pay every week, even if they are sitting around without clients. Meanwhile, you can still get permission from the people in your network to market your firm as something much bigger than yourself. For instance, you can feature the experts in your network on your website's bio page, and even market their capabilities.

You can take this idea quite far. For instance, a Silicon Valley Technology Marketing firm has developed a database of 4,000 experts they can call on anytime a client needs the proverbial needle in the haystack. They developed this database by posting ads on LinkedIn, Monster.com, and other job sites. If you visited the offices of this company, you would just see a few full-time employees. However, this company has developed expertise in quickly recruiting contractors in response to a client's needs, and negotiating fair terms for all parties involved.

There are a few key tricks to doing all of this:

- Make a commitment to constantly increase the size of your network by finding experts who complement your capabilities.

- Set up a database that you update regularly. You need to be able to keep in touch with these experts and reach them quickly when you find a potential fit.

- Keep track of who is in your network, and target clients who might benefit from your capabilities as well as those of your colleagues.

- Create a set of standards about how you set up and conduct engagements with clients, including a professional code and training in your methodologies. Everyone on your virtual team needs to be on the same page.

- Be prepared to spend time assessing and managing the client's satisfaction, especially if the engagement involves many contractors.

- Have backup contractors in place. For instance, many clients want to interview a few coaches for fit before choosing one.

- Develop contracts that protect your interests. For instance, clients should agree not to discuss the terms of your contracts with them with anyone except you. They also should agree not to hire any of your contractors without negotiating with you for a placement fee. Have your contractors agree to parallel terms, so that they don't discuss terms or solicit work directly from your clients. Most importantly, make absolutely sure that your clients pay you in the same way that you pay your contractors. Otherwise, you might find yourself short of cash. If the client pays you based on the number of hours your contractors work, it would be a huge mistake to pay your contractors a fixed fee. If you want to build a virtual firm that uses contractors, it is worth paying a contract attorney for advice and template contracts.

There are two approaches to figuring out how much you get and how much contractors get. The first is a simple formula: Whoever generates the lead and closes the deal is entitled to one-third of the contract amount. So, if you generate the lead and close the deal, you get a third of that contract. The coach who does the work gets the remaining two thirds. If someone else generates the lead and wants a finder's fee, three up to ten percent is the standard, depending on the size of the deal and your negotiating skill.

The second approach is to negotiate based on what you think you can get. For instance, suppose that the client agrees to a $10,000-per-month contract. You know that the coach who will do the work would be delighted to receive $2,000 per month for the work. Why give that coach two-thirds of this deal—over $6,000—when you only need to pay him $2,000? For instance, the leadership communication coach mentioned earlier in the book gives two-day workshops for $30,000. He subcontracts some of this work out to another coach, who happily takes $2,500 plus expenses.

It takes guts to follow the second approach, but that's how the larger firms do it. You have to get comfortable saying, "Joe, I have a great client who needs some help. I can pay you $2,000. Interested?" Joe either agrees, says no, or makes a counteroffer. If he agrees, you are in business. If he says no, find someone else who can do what Joe does, or do the work on your own. If Joe makes a counteroffer, you get to decide whether to agree, say no, or make your own counteroffer. As long as you know how much you can make from the deal, you can decide how much you are willing to pay others to get involved.

Once you get good at bringing other professionals in to work with your clients, and you have a constant flow of business, you can consider hiring full-time staff. Test out potential employees as contractors first, and confirm that you like the results they get, their attitude, and their ethics. Hire only a core staff for the minimum amount of work you know you can find, and flex up and down with contractors. From there, if you get big enough, you might even have to hire administrative help to handle recruiting experts for specific engagements and handling the contracts.

Remember: If you control the client, you control the deal. Once attracting and retaining clients becomes natural to you, you can start bringing in other coaches, consultants, and experts to do the work—while you sit back and enjoy the rewards.

Chapter Thirty

DEVELOP TOOLS FOR CLIENTS
AND FOR OTHER COACHES

A s a coach, you sit on the front lines with your clients. You get to learn about their top issues and, if you are creative, you can come up with tools to help your clients solve them—beyond coaching and other professional services. Meanwhile, you are also likely to discover ways to make it easier for you to coach clients. If you listen and observe, you will identify opportunities to develop tools that augment your coaching and help your clients solve problems. You can also develop tools that help other coaches be more effective, and market those.

One of the best places to start is by creating your own diagnostic tools. A diagnostic tool might not be as scientific as an off-the-shelf assessment, at least at first, but it can quickly point out what your clients do well, and where they have opportunities to improve. For instance, my wife Elena's etiquette program offers a 44-point business etiquette diagnostic, and an 80-point children and teen etiquette diagnostic. Each of these tools lists key etiquette behaviors—like saying please and thank you at appropriate times, or using a napkin correctly when eating—and rates how frequently the participant demonstrates those behaviors correctly. My Nurse Manager's Performance Leadership program includes a self-assessment of the key competencies required by nurses. My business-coaching program includes an in-depth business diagnostic that follows the CASTLE model for business growth. It also includes a quick, back-of-the-envelope diagnostic to make a fast decision about where to focus the coaching. We include these diagnostics with our coaching programs, sell them independently to clients, and also sell them as part of our certification programs.

You can create diagnostic tools, too. Start by making a list of the key behaviors that a successful person in your target market demonstrates. Categorize these behaviors into a few major categories so that your diagnostic is elegant. Even better, have the diagnostic follow the same logic as one of your frameworks.

Add a scale that rates the frequency or effectiveness of these behaviors. Develop a methodology to get data, whether through a self-assessment by your client or asking others for input. Suddenly, you have a diagnostic tool that you can market. Over time, you can test it out to make sure that it is accurate, and perhaps even hire a statistician to help you make it statistically valid. Once you do that, you can start collecting data about the most successful people in your target market, and continue to make the tool more valuable as a valid normative assessment.

Similarly, you can create a tool to benchmark your client against others in the market based on specific data. For instance, a healthcare consultant and coach developed an online program to benchmark a hospital's productivity compared to other, similar hospitals. The benchmark tells a hospital executive what percentile his hospital is in on a variety of dimensions, for instance: labor costs by type of inpatient unit, utilization of supplies, patient length of stay, and even overall physician productivity. He charges his clients a subscription fee to be able to use this tool on a regular basis, and has made a lot of money doing so.

Your tool doesn't have to be complex, as a tool called Schedulesmith (www.schedulesmith.com) shows. Sports coach Brad Berkowitz and his father-in-law developed it. It started when Brad's father-in-law invented a service that sent out automatic emails and text messages to his golf buddies to make sure they knew who was playing, and when. Meanwhile, Brad was becoming frustrated as a sports coach because, in his words, "It was such a pain to confirm attendance for after-work and intramural sports teams. If I didn't call or email, people would forget about the game."

Brad took his father-in-law's scheduling system and ran with it for sports teams. He shares, "I started marketing Schedulesmith to sports teams. In just over a year, I have signed up almost 15,000 users. We are now beginning to get advertising on the site, which will help us monetize it. In addition, we will soon be charging $4.95/month/team instead of offering it for free. I have spoken to several large, national companies that are interested in advertising with us going forward."

Meanwhile, Jeff Levin has taken the idea of cross-promotion and turned it into what he believes is a revolutionary service called GrowthPOD (www.GrowthPOD.com). GrowthPOD allows businesses to co-promote each other through their social networking site as well as through newsletters, using a form of promotion that Jeff has coined Co-Opvertising. He explains, "Third-party endorsements work—that's why companies ask celebrities to endorse their products. Although most of our alliances aren't with national celebrities, they are with influential experts in their field and in our target area. They have built relationships with each customer on their list, who value and trust their opinion. Our system allows people to benefit from their relationships and gain valuable and inexpensive endorsement-quality exposure, which leads to more leads. The beauty is that we do it in a way that never exposes any client information."

Marian Thier, CEO of Expanding Thought, Inc., developed *Hear! Hear? Your Listening Portfolio* and a new line of business, Listening Impact, for clients. For her, the opportunity came from a simple realization: "A few years ago, I noticed that there was a pattern among my coaching clients that was a major factor in their career derailment as well as in poor decision-making—they do not listen."

She continues, "I set about doing a lot of research and discovered that there are different modes of listening that influence what someone pays attention to and what they leave on the table unheard. When I couldn't find a way to help clients understand how they listen and how that impacts their effectiveness, I developed *Hear! Hear?* Now listening is an extension to my business, with coach certification, webinar and workshop, blog, domain name, logo, and website. Results so far: Over 300 people have taken the assessment, we've conducted a half dozen webinars and even more workshops, and we continue to get repeat and new orders. There are also over a dozen certified practitioners. I predict the revenue from Listening Impact will soon surpass the other Expanding Thought, Inc. income."

There are many other examples of tools for coaches and clients to use. For instance, Kim Ades, MBA, President and Owner of Frame of Mind Coaching, licenses her JournalEngine coaching platform (www.journalengine.com), a platform she describes as "leveraging the power of journaling in a simple and cost-effective way, helping coaches create and provide a deeper, more meaningful engagement with their clients."

Mindjet (www.mindjet.com) is another online tool for coaches that enables professionals to visually connect ideas, information, and people. It is a useful tool for brainstorming, mind mapping, plotting strategy, and managing processes—in short, many of the things that coaches work on with clients.

Other ideas include: developing web templates for your clients, or for your fellow coaches; developing reporting software for clients to track results and be accountable; creating and marketing a directory of experts in your client's industry or your field; and helping coaches publish books, develop information products, and put on seminars.

You can develop tools like these by asking some simple questions:

- What are the things that I do manually with clients over and over again, and that I could be doing more efficiently if I had an automated tool?

- What are situations in which clients say, "Gee, I wish I had that information at my fingertips... How can I find out what I need to know quickly and easily?"

- What are products I can offer to coaches and clients to help them get more business?

- If I could create any type of tool to help my clients get results beyond what coaching can provides, what tool would that be?

- What are the top complaints of my clients? How can I make at least one of those complaints go away?

- What are the top complaints of other coaches and trusted advisors? How can I make at least one of those complaints go away?

- How can I create solutions to help coaches create million-dollar firms, for instance, by creating leverage through products and other people?

Chapter Thirty-One

CREATE A CENTER OF EXCELLENCE OR AN INSTITUTE

I f you have implemented even one suggestion from this part of the book, you are already way ahead of most coaches. Congratulations!

Now take one final step: Create a center of excellence or an institute. As with developing certification programs, there is no special magic to it. If others can do it, so can you. All you have to do is realize that you are worthy of having a center or an institute, be willing to declare it, and then make it happen through equal parts marketing and strong execution.

Why not you? Why do other experts get to start an institute but not you? Assuming you have the expertise, a network of people who view you as credible, a series of programs to offer, and an ongoing commitment to learn about and disseminate best practices, you have what it takes.

Take a moment and imagine that you ran an institute or center of excellence based on your unique expertise. Answer these questions:

- What do you call your institute?

- Which programs do you offer, including: coaching, group coaching, consulting, assessments, books, CDs, DVDs, information products, leadership circles, consulting, training, seminars, and speaking?

- What types of free information do you provide to establish your credibility?

- What does your website look like?

- Who else is involved on your board of advisors, or as contributors, to build some social proof?

In many ways, we are right back at the beginning of where you started as a coach. You are an expert who provides coaching as one of many ways to solve your clients' most pressing problems, and to help them get results. An institute or center of excellence is merely the culmination of your expertise. It is an umbrella body that solidifies all of the ways in which you demonstrate your expertise and dominate your niche as a true thought leader and advisor.

You don't have to start big. As you read earlier, my Center for Executive Coaching started out as nothing more than a single web page. Now people from around the world contact me to train them, or their people, to become executive-level coaches. Start small, and grow your institute over time.

Step VI

CREATE YOUR MILLION-DOLLAR BUSINESS PLAN

None of the first five steps matter if you don't make a plan and commit to taking action to make it happen. Now the rubber hits the road. It is time for you to take action and realize your true potential as a coach. This starts by coming up with your unique million-dollar business model. Then you need a practical, achievable action plan to gain momentum and make your million-dollar business model happen. Remember: Action makes things happen. Even small actions can get you visible to prospects, and people who know prospects, and open up doors on the way to much bigger success.

Chapter Thirty-Two

YOUR MILLION-DOLLAR BUSINESS MODEL

There are many ways to skin a cat, many ways to reach the top of a mountain, and many ways to build a million-dollar firm. It all depends on the types of clients you choose to serve, the types of programs you offer, and how you decide to build leverage in your practice. Every successful coach has done it differently. You have to blaze your own trail.

It is also difficult to predict how your business will change over time. As you gain confidence, build your network, and refine your marketing message and strategies, you will likely move up the food chain to higher-paying clients and engagements. Meanwhile, it is likely that you will see the share of your revenue from different sources change. For instance, one or more of your information products might take off and eclipse coaching as your primary revenue source. Or, maybe other forms of services to clients—like strategic retreats, training programs, consulting, and leadership circles—generate an increasing share of your revenues and get you to the million-dollar mark. You could bring in contractors and employees and, even as they build your revenues and give you financial leverage, they could also introduce new service offerings. It's possible they'll help you get into new markets. As long as you stay active and keep testing new ways to serve clients and grow your business, good things will happen.

For the above reasons, the purpose of this chapter is not to give you a one-size-fits-all business model for your coaching business. That's impossible. Rather, the chapter points out different possibilities for you and encourages you to come up with scenarios that will help you achieve your goals. Let's break your business model down into segments: the direct client services you provide, the client services that others provide on your behalf, and the products that give you leverage.

DIRECT CLIENT SERVICES THAT YOU PROVIDE.

The business model for direct client services is straightforward: How much does each client pay you? How much do you want to make, and how many clients do you need to achieve that goal?

Some coaches are highly disciplined and efficient in their coaching. They run something akin to a coaching factory. At the extreme, coaches who follow this model dedicate three or four days per week to coaching clients. They coach one hour at a time, usually by phone or by having clients come to their office. Clients come to the coach one after another, like a factory assembly line. The coach reserves the remaining one or two days to market his practice and develop new coaching programs and products. If the coach has any extra capacity, he uses that time to find new clients until his practice is full again. Meanwhile, a coach starting out with this model spends every spare minute getting visible and attracting clients until he has a full roster.

To illustrate this model, assume that the coach can work with six clients per day, and sees each client weekly. In this example, he can work with up to 24 clients per month. If he provides group coaching or provides other types of professional services to clients, he needs to reduce this number to make time for those services, too. Once the coach starts to exceed the time he has available for clients, he needs to train other coaches to take on client work on his behalf.

Other coaches have a more relaxed approach and often end up making more money than those who run coaching factories. These coaches take on fewer clients by focusing on wealthy individuals and top executives at midsized to large firms. These top-tier clients pay the high end on the range of coaching fees. Additionally, many of these clients will pay you these fees without needing to meet with you on a weekly basis. Their time is valuable, and if they can get terrific results from you in a single meeting per month instead of through weekly meetings, they see that as a good thing. This frees up even more of your time to develop products, hire other professionals, and go after other big clients.

To reach this point, you need to move up the food chain as a coach and as a credible expert. By following the advice so far in this book, you can do this. It takes a simple choice—the choice to target people at these levels, understand their top issues, develop valuable solutions to their problems, and take action to reach out to them. Demonstrate to your clients that you are credible and get results.

From here, you can offer a full range of services to your clients, whether by doing it yourself or by bringing in other experts. Coaching gets you in the door, and is a starting point to expand your presence with each and every client. Once your clients see you as a credible expert, and you build a trusting relationship, they will want more access to your expertise. It becomes much easier to sell additional services, because your clients trust you and want to share their problems with you. You can offer them a range of services to solve those problems: consulting, training, facilitating strategy sessions, joining leadership circles, bringing in other experts, and perhaps even serving as an interim executive. You are a true trusted advisor capable of wearing multiple hats to help your clients succeed.

Take a moment and think about your direct services model. How many clients can you handle every week or month? How much do you expect to earn from a typical client over a year, including coaching and all other professional services? Given these numbers, how much in annual revenues can you expect from providing direct services to clients?

As you can guess, the range is all over the map. It depends on your target market, whether you have low- or high-pricing self-esteem, and how aggressive you are with business development. I know coaches who think that asking a client for $500 per month is a terrifying step, and others who won't take a client for less than $100,000 for a yearlong engagement. You have to do some research in your market, give yourself a gut check, and choose the pricing that works for you. From there, choose how many clients you feel comfortable working with before you have to bring in other coaches to help you out. That will give you an estimate of how much money you can earn every year from direct client work.

Alternatively, start with an income goal and work your way backwards. Assuming an average fee per client engagement, how many clients do you need in order to hit that goal? For instance, if you want to earn $500,000, and you know that you can make $25,000 per client engagement per year, then you need to attract 20 clients.

Play with some different scenarios until you come up with a low number that seems relatively easy to achieve, and a stretch number that is aggressive.

CLIENT SERVICES THAT OTHERS PROVIDE.

You read earlier that there are two ways to make money by bringing other professionals into your client engagements. The first is to claim one-third of the fee that you charge clients. The second is to negotiate the best margin you can.

For the purposes of this exercise, keep it simple and assume you will claim one-third of the fee for any client you bring in.

If you want to generate leverage through other professionals, set a goal and work backwards to figure out what this means for your business. For instance, if you want to completely replace your own income with outsourced contractors, you need to market the equivalent of three full-time people. If you want to earn $150,000 through outsourced contractors, you need to market $450,000 worth of engagements.

PRODUCTS THAT CREATE LEVERAGE FOR YOU.

Some products you create and market will bomb, some will do okay, and a few might take off. You never know until you take action. For now, choose the products that interest you the most and that seem to have the most potential, given your interests and target market. Make a commitment to choose at least one and develop it. At the same time, estimate how much you might charge for any of these products, and how many you need to sell to make the products a significant part of your business model.

Use the chart below. For each product that interests you, take a stab at what's possible. If you have no idea about what to charge, do some research into similar products both within and outside your target market. For volume assumptions, play with low, medium, and high scenarios based on the number of people in your niche. Just play, and see what becomes possible!

Product Type	Your Specific Idea	(A) Potential Units Sold Per Year	(B) Price Per Unit	Total Potential Revenues (A X B)
Books				
Information Products				
Seminars				
Subscriptions				

Product Type	Your Specific Idea	(A) Potential Units Sold Per Year	(B) Price Per Unit	Total Potential Revenues (A X B)
Leadership Circles				
Certifications				
Licensing Deals				
Tools for clients and other coaches				
Other Ideas				
Potential Total				

Now put the above three revenue sources together. Write down your totals in the table below:

Source of Revenue	$ Revenue
Target revenue from direct client work:	
Target revenue from leverage via other professionals:	
Target revenue from products:	
Total target revenues:	

How much do you expect to earn from each source? What percentage of your total revenues does each source contribute? Are you satisfied with your targets? If not, keep adjusting until you have something that seems aggressive but achievable, and that reaches your goals.

Chapter Thirty-Three

YOUR ACTION PLAN

n the previous chapter, you defined your business model. Now it is time to take action to achieve your goals and make your business model a reality.

It used to be fashionable to set specific goals and break them down into a linear set of manageable chunks to achieve them. While that is a useful exercise, recent research shows that this is not always the best way to achieve your goals. For instance, John Kay's book, *Obliquity: Why Our Goals are Best Achieved Indirectly*, suggests that a meandering path is often the best way. My own experience with building a firm, along with those of my colleagues, seems to follow a combination of both approaches. On the one hand, you have to keep taking action to be visible in your market, build your credibility, keep evolving in the ways that you serve clients, and make things happen. On the other hand, you can't predict exactly which clients and business opportunities will come your way while you do all of this. But you can anticipate, and be prepared for, opportunities when they appear—and you can be assured that taking effective action will make all sorts of good things come your way.

For instance, I never would have predicted that I'd be writing a book with one of my business heroes, Jay Conrad Levinson. However, when a colleague of mine introduced me to him, I was ready to pitch some ideas. This has resulted in a phenomenally valuable collaboration for both of us.

Therefore, the goal of this chapter is to have you create an action plan to take some immediate next steps, build momentum, and keep growing from there. Your action plan depends on where you are right now as a coach. There are three possibilities: you are just starting out and need your first client; you have clients but not a full practice; or you have a full practice and now need to build leverage through other people and products. Following is a suggested action plan for each of these situations.

FOR THE COACH WHO IS JUST STARTING OUT.

If you are new and have no clients, your goal is crystal clear: Get your first client. Don't let anything distract you from this goal. You don't need to write a book. You don't need to produce a glossy brochure announcing your services. You don't need to create a database of potential contractors. You need to focus on getting clients the way a cat focuses on catching prey.

Your action plan is simple. It will feel as though you are pushing a boulder up a hill while you implement it. Prepare for this feeling, and get to work:

1. Choose your target market.

2. Understand the needs of the market.

3. Develop at least one coaching framework and methodology to solve a major problem that the people in your market face.

4. Write a compelling marketing message that describes your value in a compelling way. Use the earlier parts of this book as a reference.

5. Get advice about your marketing message from people you trust and who know your market, and refine it based on their advice.

6. Develop a clear pricing strategy, so that if someone has interest, you can close the deal on the spot.

7. Write down a list of everyone you know who might be able to make introductions for you.

8. Get out there and get introductions.

9. After you have some momentum with the above steps, get a website with a blog, populate your blog, build up your social media presence, and start looking for ways to educate your market through speaking, seminars, and writing.

10. Use every single failure as a way to learn how to get better. If you feel like giving up, don't. Instead, take one more step. Then another, and another, and another. Eventually you will gain momentum.

FOR THE COACH WHO HAS CLIENTS BUT NOT A FULL PRACTICE.

You have a dual action plan. First, turbocharge your business development activities so that you can continue to fill your practice.

Second, if you haven't already, start building leverage in your practice. You have to decide whether to start with leverage through products, leverage through other people, or both simultaneously. If you want to begin with products, I suggest that you choose a type of product from the ideas in this book. There will be something that suits you, from writing a book to developing an information product, launching a seminar, or creating a leadership circle made up of your existing clients. Carve out some time and make it happen. Once you do, you have a source of leverage in your practice, as well as an asset, that will serve you well for the rest of your career. I guarantee it.

Many coaches get in their own way when it comes to creating that first product. If this describes you, get your own coach and be more coachable with this person than you ever have been in your life. You are leaving money, status, and credibility on the table when you don't take advantage of the opportunity to create information products.

If you are really stuck, create the easiest product you can. Interview some industry thought leaders on a recorded line and turn those interviews into a CD or an eBook. Get someone to videotape you giving a speech, and turn that into a DVD. Give a series of free telecalls to the people on your list; record the calls and sell the recordings. Do not procrastinate. Do not cave in. Do it, now.

At the same time, if it is part of your vision for your practice, prepare to start bringing other people in to your client engagements. Develop a list of the types of complementary professionals and coaches with whom you can form alliances, and start reaching out to the appropriate people. Meanwhile, think about the types of clients and client engagements where you can bring in other professionals. Develop a plan to reach out to those clients, or to expand your presence with your existing clients by bringing in a team.

FOR THE COACH WHO HAS A FULL PRACTICE AND NEEDS LEVERAGE.

If you have a full practice, congratulations are in order. However, it is now time to take the next step and build leverage. You have two choices and, depending on your preferences and aspirations, you can choose one or both of them.

First, follow the advice above and start creating information products. Most importantly, don't let yourself be overwhelmed. Pick one idea and test it out. Then pick another. Keep building on what works and learn from what doesn't.

If you already have some leverage through products, but not enough, choose an idea with a high price tag and test that out. Many coaches roll out CDs and DVDs, and need to add higher-priced products to their portfolio—products like high-end information programs, certifications, licensing opportunities, seminars, and leadership circles.

Second, take advantage of your business development skills. Start marketing other coaches, consultants, and experts to your clients—and earn a profit in the process. Follow the advice already provided in this book to make that happen. For instance, create a contract for clients and contractors. Develop a set of professional standards for anyone who works with you. If appropriate, prepare a training system to get contractors up to speed on your approach to coaching. Start with just one contractor. If it works out, build on your success and keep moving forward. If that contractor doesn't work out, don't give up. Learn from the experience and do better with the next one.

The key for you is to start creating a firm right now. If you don't, you might make a decent living, but you will only have a job. If anything happens to you, your firm stops cold. If you want to retire, you give up the wealth you could have had by selling your business. I don't know whether you have a family that relies on you or not, but if you do, you owe it to them to create wealth by building a real firm. If you don't have a family, you still have an obligation to make sure your retirement is secure.

For the coach with a full practice and no leverage, it can be hard to take that first step. You have to carve out time to build leverage. Of course, that could potentially cut into time and revenue from clients. You might even see your revenues slip for a bit. However, making this choice pays off in the long run. Invest some time and money now to get back much more time, and money, later.

What are you waiting for? Regardless of which of the above three situations is the most applicable to you, read the conclusion to this book, then get out there, and take one small step towards your million-dollar firm.

Conclusion

CLAIM YOUR POWER AS A COACH

I t surprises me how many coaches don't claim their own power. We are trained to help others overcome their limiting beliefs, take action to achieve their most ambitious aspirations, and be more successful in life and at work. Yet many coaches fail to embrace the same wisdom and insights they help their clients receive. When it comes to their coaching practices, many coaches think too small and barely make enough money to get by.

Not you. Not anymore. Remember: You are an expert. You have insights and wisdom that are extremely valuable. You are passionate about helping people make amazing things happen, and you know how to get them from point A to a better point B. Claim your power. Share your expertise. Realize how much value you can contribute. Think big! Reach as many people as you possibly can. To do otherwise is selfish and stingy.

- Who says you can't fill your practice with desirable, high-paying clients? You can.

- Who says you can't establish yourself as the go-to professional in your niche, the one people call first when they have a pressing problem? You can.

- Who says you can't form alliances with major players in your target market, so that you generate a stream of clients? You can.

- Who says you can't charge the high fees that you deserve, based on the value you provide? You can.

- Who says you can't have your clients come back again and again for your services, while raving about you to others? You can.

- Who says you can't write a book, or books, and become a recognized expert? You can.

- Who says you can't sell information products that let people solve their problems on their own—and then contact you if they need more help? You can.

- Who says you can't bring the leaders in your field together and have them pay you to facilitate meetings among them? You can.

- Who says you can't certify others in your methodologies in exchange for a new income stream? You can.

- Who says you can't license your content and enjoy a stream of ongoing revenues? You can.

- Who says you can't bring others into your client engagements, so that you make money while doing other things? You can.

- Who says you can't create a million-dollar firm? You can!

Claim your power as a coach. Take one small step every day to move forward. Treat yourself as your best coaching client, and give yourself compassion, guidance, and a kick in the pants as, and when, needed. Start this very moment. Pick one piece of advice in this book that you know will benefit your coaching practice, and take action, right now, to make it happen. Get going.

Meanwhile, keep me posted on your progress. You can always reach me through The Center for Executive Coaching at www.centerforexecutivecoaching. com. Best of success!

ABOUT THE AUTHORS

Jay Conrad Levinson is the author of history's best-selling marketing series, "Guerrilla Marketing," plus 58 other business books. His books have sold more than 21 million copies worldwide. His guerrilla concepts have influenced marketing so much that his books appear in 62 languages and are required reading in MBA programs worldwide.

He was born in Detroit, raised in Chicago, and graduated from the University of Colorado. His studies in Psychology led him to advertising agencies, including a Directorship at Leo Burnett in London, where he served as Creative Director. Returning to the USA, he joined J. Walter Thompson as Senior VP. Jay created and taught Guerrilla Marketing for ten years at the extension division of the University of California in Berkeley.

A winner of first prizes in all the media, he has been part of the creative teams that made household names of The Marlboro Man, The Pillsbury Doughboy, Allstate's good hands, United's friendly skies, the Sears Diehard battery, Morris the Cat, Mr. Clean, Tony the Tiger, and the Jolly Green Giant.

Today, Guerrilla Marketing is the most powerful brand in the history of marketing, listed among the 100 best business books ever written, and is now a popular website at www.gmarketing.com. It also powers The Guerrilla Marketing Association—a support system for small business.

Although Jay is able to list those notable accomplishments, he believes that the most notable is that, since 1971, he has worked a three-day week from his home.

After living in the San Francisco Bay Area for 35 years, Jay and Jeannie Levinson sold their home, bought an RV, and towed a Jeep. They ended up, six years later, at their lakefront home outside Orlando, Florida, and close to their 26 grandchildren, their own personal Disney World. Nobody on earth is as qualified to tell you about Guerrilla Marketing as the Father of Guerrilla Marketing, Jay Conrad Levinson.

Andrew Neitlich runs a successful coaching and consulting practice and is a leading trainer of executive-level coaches. His coaching practice focuses on leaders in emerging technology, healthcare, universities, non-profits, and professional services firms. He is also the founder and director of The Center for Executive Coaching (www.centerforexecutivecoaching.com), The Institute for Business Growth (www.instituteforbusinessgrowth.com), and The Center for Career Coaching (www.centerforcareercoaching.com). These organizations train coaches and aspiring coaches from around the world to work with executives and business owners.

He is also the executive director of Solo Revolution (www.solorevolution.com), a unique association of solopreneurs from around the world who are building businesses and living life on their terms. Andrew received his undergraduate degree from Harvard College in 1987, and his MBA from Harvard Business School in 1991. He lives with his wife, Elena, and three children (Noah, Seth, and Willow) in Sarasota, Florida, where he plays tennis almost every day.

TO LEARN MORE ABOUT ANDREW NEITLICH AND HOW TO BECOME A TOP-TIER EXECUTIVE-LEVEL COACH, VISIT:

www.CenterforExecutiveCoaching.com

www.InstituteforBusinessGrowth.com

www.CenterforCareerCoaching.com

For more insights about how to grow your coaching practice, visit:

www.SoloRevolution.com

TO LEARN MORE ABOUT GUERRILLA MARKETING AND JAY CONRAD LEVINSON, VISIT

www.gmarketing.com.

BUY A SHARE OF THE FUTURE IN YOUR COMMUNITY

These certificates make great holiday, graduation and birthday gifts that can be personalized with the recipient's name. The cost of one S.H.A.R.E. or one square foot is $54.17. The personalized certificate is suitable for framing and will state the number of shares purchased and the amount of each share, as well as the recipient's name. The home that you participate in "building" will last for many years and will continue to grow in value.

Here is a sample SHARE certificate:

THIS CERTIFIES THAT

YOUR NAME HERE

HAS INVESTED IN A HOME FOR A DESERVING FAMILY

1985-2010

TWENTY-FIVE YEARS OF BUILDING FUTURES
IN OUR COMMUNITY ONE HOME AT A TIME

1200 SQUARE FOOT HOUSE @ $65,000 = $54.17 PER SQUARE FOOT
This certificate represents a tax deductible donation. It has no cash value.

YES, I WOULD LIKE TO HELP!

*I support the work that Habitat for Humanity does and I want to be part of the excitement! As a donor, I will receive periodic updates on your construction activities but, more importantly, I know my gift will help a family in our community realize the dream of homeownership. **I would like to SHARE in your efforts against substandard housing in my community!** (Please print below)*

PLEASE SEND ME _____ SHARES at $54.17 EACH = $ $_____

In Honor Of: _____

Occasion: (Circle One)   *HOLIDAY*   *BIRTHDAY*   *ANNIVERSARY*

　　　　　OTHER: _____

Address of Recipient: _____

Gift From: _____ *Donor Address:* _____

Donor Email: _____

I AM ENCLOSING A CHECK FOR $ $_____ PAYABLE TO HABITAT FOR HUMANITY <u>OR</u> PLEASE CHARGE MY VISA OR MASTERCARD *(CIRCLE ONE)*

Card Number _____ Expiration Date: _____

Name as it appears on Credit Card _____ Charge Amount $ _____

Signature _____

Billing Address _____

Telephone # Day _____ Eve _____

PLEASE NOTE: Your contribution is tax-deductible to the fullest extent allowed by law.
Habitat for Humanity • P.O. Box 1443 • Newport News, VA 23601 • 757-596-5553
www.HelpHabitatforHumanity.org

CPSIA information can be obtained at www.ICGtesting.com
Printed in the USA
BVOW05s1450250315

393321BV00005B/198/P